Poverty and the Social Context of Sex Work in Addis Ababa

An Anthropological Perspective

Bethlehem Tekola

Forum for Social Studies
Addis Ababa

FSS Special Monograph Series 2

Financial support for this publication has been provided by the
FSS donor consortium, which consists of the Norwegian Embassy,
Netherlands Embassy, DFID and the Irish Embassy.

ISBN 1-904855-67-9
ISBN-13: 978-1-904855-67-5

Text Layout by Mihret Demissew

This book is dedicated to the loving memory of:

> My father, Tekola Gebru, whose confidence in me has been
> perpetually inspiring;
> My mother, Aberash Habte-Mariam, whose care was nurturing
> and her innocence regrettable;
> My sister, Hanna Tekola, by whose friendship I was comforted and
> in whose name I have promised.

Table of Contents

Acknowledgements

This book has grown out of my MA thesis. I am indebted to the Addis Ababa University School of Graduate Studies, the Center for Research, Training and Information on Women in Development (CERTWID) of Addis Ababa University and the Graduate School of Asian and African Area Studies (ASAFAS) of Kyoto University, Japan, for generously funding the fieldwork and write-up of the thesis. I would also like to express my gratitude for the intellectual guidance I received from my MA thesis advisor, Dr. Alula Pankhurst. I appreciate greatly his advice on both substantive and technical matters.

To all the women who have generously taken time to answer my seemingly endless questions about their lives, I have no words with which to repay their patience and understanding. To the best of my recollection, not one of them has failed the test of friendship, decency and deep humanity. I am grateful to them for proving me right in conceiving a research agenda that envisaged stating this very fact about them.

Last but by no means least I would like to express my sincere thanks and appreciation to Professor Bahru Zewde of the Department of History of Addis Ababa University and Dessalegn Rahmato of the Forum for Social Studies (FSS) for their work in editing this book and for their constant encouragement and cooperation in the publication of my MA thesis.

This book is dedicated to my parents, Tekola Gebru and Aberash H/Mariam, to my sister Hanna Tekola and to all women who have confided to me the most intimate stories of their lives.

Abstract

This book explores the social context of sex work in the city of Addis Ababa. It focuses on the social ties between sex workers and a variety of other categories of people, from their family members to their relatives, from their roommates to their neighbors, from their coworkers to their clients. It explores which of these social ties are affirmed and reinforced, which come under strain and which are cultivated and built by the women as a result of their engagement in sex work. It argues that these things depend on the women's background, on the conditions under which they turn to sex work, on the specific types and conditions of sex work that they do and on the places and conditions of their residence. The main thesis of the work is that sex workers share the same social milieu and value system with non-sex workers and that, despite severe constraints put on them by poverty and very difficult working conditions, they struggle on a daily basis to have social life and social relevance. The work critiques the very common castigation of sex workers as social misfits who pose dangers to society and proposes a humane approach towards them and their dependents, an approach that should begin by making a clear distinction between the institution of commercial sex and the women who practice it.

The work employs both qualitative and quantitative methodology. It combines detailed one-to-one interviewing with focus group discussions and personal observation to bring out the perspectives of the women themselves. The quantitative data is composed of responses to a structured questionnaire by 100 sex workers.

The book begins with a critical review of existing literature on commercial sex work. The review establishes that in the West, in Africa, as well as in Ethiopia, sex workers have often been conflated with sex work itself; that they have been described either as sick and immoral people or as victims of male domination and abuse; and that they are described as such in categorical terms, without any attempt at internally differentiating among them.

The book then suggests a scheme for a classification of the sex workers of Addis Ababa. The scheme is based on those variables that determine the terms and conditions of social interaction between the women and wider society. They include the women's backgrounds, the circumstances of their entry into sex work, the terms and conditions of work, the terms and conditions of residence and the degree and forms of dependent relationships in which they are involved. The analysis of sex work in Addis Ababa on the basis of these variables suggests significant shifts in the social background of the women who engage in it as well as in the organization of the work. The fourth chapter of the book employs this scheme and works out a classification of the sex worker population in the city. Seven distinct types of sex work are identified. The organization of work and residence in each of the types is discussed, followed by descriptions of the general profile of the women who operate in each type. Finally, the implication of this classification for the social behavior of the women is discussed.

Key words: Addis Ababa, sex work, sex workers, prostitution, prostitutes, social ties, identity, morality, patriarchy, feminism, differentiation, migration, housing.

Chapter One

Introduction

1 Work, Identity and Social Life among Commercial Sex Workers in Addis Ababa

Historically, the onset of the modern age in human history (at least in the West) has been associated with increasing social differentiation and specialization of functions. Society became increasingly complex because global trade and industrialization brought about the decline of the primordial order in which rank and status were determined by birth and replaced it by a merit-based order that produced new and increasingly dynamic forms of inequality. Likewise, what humans had to do to make a living, to satisfy their curiosities, or just to pass time, came to take extremely diverse forms (Laslett, 1965; Stearns, 1977; Huppert, 1986). It can be said that one of the outcomes of these twin phenomena is the decline, if not the total disappearance, of direct association of work with identity or with personal behavior. Today, there is no such thing as the typical behavior of a businessperson, of an executive, of a worker, of a soldier or of a farmer, be they male or female, Chinese, American or German; certainly not to the extent that pre-modern societies spoke of the social behaviors of patricians, plebeians, princes, princesses, lords, peasants or slaves.

It is remarkable, therefore, that contrary to trends in all other occupations, modernity actually came to be characterized by the establishment of a direct relationship between livelihood, on the one hand, and social identity and behavior, on the other, when it comes to women who engage in one category of work: commercial sex. It is also remarkable that this association has come to endure. There is a very strong belief that the identity as well as the social personality of women who engage in commercial sex is defined by what they do to earn their living. "Prostitution", more than any other line of work, is believed to determine group identity, whether such identity is accepted by the women or simply ascribed to them. It is also believed that "prostitution" defines the attitudes, the behaviors or the overall personality of each woman even when she is not at work. These beliefs are all the more striking because public commentators, scholars and activists who subscribe to them (in

1

some cases openly, in others only indirectly) reflect and represent perspectives that can be described as polar opposites of each other. What these perspectives have produced is a difference of opinion on the question of whether "their" identity or "their" behaviors necessarily put "prostitutes" at odds with society. There is no difference of opinion on "the fact" that "prostitutes" in a given society share identities and behaviors that directly come from what they do to earn money.

In this book I will explore this intriguing phenomenon as it relates to contemporary Ethiopia. My task is to see if there is any direct connection between what commercial sex workers do to make money and the way they conduct themselves in society or relate to other people. I undertake this exploration in the temporally and spatially limited context of contemporary Addis Ababa with a sample of slightly over 100 female sex workers.

In Ethiopia, as elsewhere, public and scholarly views on commercial sex have for very long taken it for granted that "prostitution" implies distinct forms of identity, attitude and behavior. Very often, no distinction is made between the work and the women who do the work to earn a living. Moreover, in Ethiopia, public as well as scholarly perceptions of "prostitutes" as a group have always portrayed them as social misfits and their supposed attitudes and behaviors are described always as inimical to society. More recently, under the threat posed by the HIV/AIDS phenomenon, this identification of sex work with social misfits imbued with dangerous social personalities and personal traits has become even more categorical and insistent. The result has been that public and government perceptions of the connections between commercial sex and health problems have been equally categorical and not sufficiently informed. The interventions based on these perceptions, even when genuinely meant to help both the women and the rest of society, have likewise not been as effective as they might have been.

In this work I approach the problem outlined above in two stages. The first stage is that of analysis in which I will explore the historical and methodological basis of the problem through an extended review of past and current literature on commercial sex in Ethiopia and elsewhere. I will show how notions about "prostitute" identity, attitude and behavior have persisted despite the variety of angles from which commercial sex has been approached in the West as well as in Africa. The second stage is that of describing my own approach to the problem, to be followed by a presentation of my research findings. Here, I will outline my conscious shift of perspective and methodology and present an alternative view suggested to me by research among the women concerned.

2   A Humane Approach to Commercial Sex -Workers and their Dependents

Students of commercial sex have always faced the inherent contradictions (mostly potential contradictions but also real ones) between critically examining commercial sex as such and protecting or working for the rights of the women who practice it (Barry, 1981b, 1984; O'Neill, 1994). Given the high degree of sensitivity created by the HIV/AIDS pandemic, I also feel compelled to state a disclaimer about this work before I describe its significance. I wish to state very clearly that *this work is not an effort to rehabilitate commercial sex in the view of the public or of academia!* On the contrary, it is meant to call attention to a dimension of the problem that should not be overlooked in any effort to reduce, regulate or eliminate the practice! This dimension is what I would like to call *the human dimension*, in which the women who practice commercial sex and the people who depend on their earnings for their sustenance are distinguished from the practice itself.

Time and again one hears of programs or initiatives to eliminate or regulate commercial sex. Time and again the human cost of these initiatives is not taken into consideration. These initiatives are often spontaneous and are carried out with urgency and speed. For this reason, and because they are driven by the need to combat the perceived ill effects of the practice on society, they almost always do not differentiate between the practice and the practitioners. Above all, they do not consider the large number of invisible people who are sustained by the proceeds from commercial sex: the children, the siblings, the spouses, the poor parents and the relatives of the women. Drastic measures that seek to "clean out" commercial sex from a neighborhood, a zone or a street often mean "cleaning out" the women; they often mean attacking them physically or harassing them in one form or another. In the city of Addis Ababa today, these kinds of activities take place on a daily basis. I have myself witnessed several cases.

This study is significant because it will bring to light the human dimensions of the commercial sex sector in Addis Ababa. It will describe the social fabric that is sustained by income from commercial sex. It will also describe the perceptions and the feelings of the women who practice commercial sex: their pains and frustrations as well as their hopes and expectations. By so doing, the study will bring to our attention the simple but often forgotten fact that behind commercial sex are women who are mothers, sisters, daughters, relatives, neighbors and friends of the very people that we want to protect from the ills of "prostitution". In the final analysis, the principal objective, and thus the main significance, of the study will be to encourage compassionate and humane approaches toward commercial sex workers both by the public and the state, whatever it may be that they want to do with commercial sex work.

2.1 Methodology

My approach to the social context of "prostitution" in Addis Ababa is informed by methodological traditions associated with social anthropology and the Women's Movement. Although social anthropology shares in the general social science approach that combines both qualitative and quantitative research, it is noted for its ethnographic tradition that emphasizes the study of actual situations and specificities rather than of types and impersonal institutions. In Ethiopia, the study of commercial sex has for long been a favorite topic of sociologists and epidemiologists whose methodologies tended to put more emphasis on the collection and interpretation of quantitative data rather than qualitative data (Meyer, 1963; Mihretu, 1984; Lishan, 1985, Andargatchew, 1988).

Real life experiences and real people did not figure much in such studies except in the form of brief statements of responses to specific questions, often by nameless respondents. The most extensively used tool of research was the sample survey questionnaire, often developed to test existing models or theories about commercial sex or sex workers or to measure the spread or intensity of a particular problem associated with the practice. The sociological approach has thus tended to be more suited to institutional studies of commercial sex than for studies that seek to bring forward the human stories that have surrounded and continue to surround the practice. They are not quite suited, therefore, for the kind of study that I envisage here.

The anthropology of commercial sex thus requires the combined use of the techniques of research that social anthropology as a discipline has been particularly associated with: in-depth one-to-one interviews, discussions with representative samples of informants as focus groups, personal observation and sample survey. For the study of commercial sex in Addis Ababa, its merits have been demonstrated by the pioneering work of Laketch Dirasse (1978; 1991). My work will build upon Laketch's approach but will shift the emphasis somewhat to qualitative research and thus to real life situations so as to bring into sharper focus the social context of commercial sex.

Since the late 1960s and early 70s, scholarly perspectives associated with the Women's Movement have encouraged an approach to the study of commercial sex with sensitivity to the views of the women themselves (McLeod, 1982; Bujra, 1975; White, 1990; O'Neill, 1996; Phoenix, 1999). Commercial sex workers have consequently become subjects and participants rather than mere objects of study. In some cases, in fact, partnerships had been developed between scholars and sex workers themselves in which agendas are shared and strategies for advancing the agendas jointly worked out. This shift in perspective is, of course, associated with shifts in the themes and issues of interest to students of commercial sex: away from "social problems" believed to have been connected with the practice, to the problems faced by the women themselves; from issues like regulation or suppression of commercial sex, to such issues as the human and citizenship rights of sex workers, etc. Perspectives obtained from this "women-centered approach" (O'Neill, 1996) are presented sometimes in the form of life stories and sometimes as sex workers' views of particular issues related to their lives and work (Phoenix, 1999).

In this study I combine the social anthropological techniques with the women-centered approach to bring out the dimensions of commercial sex that have attracted little attention before. I also build on my own previous experience with a historical study of "prostitution" in Addis Ababa through life stories of individual women (Bethlehem, 2002). What follows is a description of the procedure I followed to exploit the possibilities offered by this combination of perspectives and techniques.

3 Preliminary Explorations

I started research by establishing contact and engaging in informal conversation with a broad variety of sex workers. I found many of them through friends and some through NGOs who work with them. I took notes in these preliminary explorations, but only occasionally and in a rather cursory fashion. My focus was on establishing rapport with the women, on informing myself as much as I could about their main concerns, and on interesting them in my project to the best of my ability. Interestingly, I quickly learnt that commercial sex workers in Addis Ababa were in a state of what can be called "researcher fatigue". Many of them reacted to my requests for cooperation with a tired "here-we-go-again" sort of response, telling me that they have responded to an endless number of researchers about HIV/AIDS and condom use. Many advised me to go find those researchers or their reports. It took some time for me to convince many of them of the difference between what I wanted to do and what previous researchers were after, or to convince them that I was a student and not a researcher for an NGO. Fortunately, most of them responded positively as soon as they learnt that I was mostly interested in their daily lives rather than in HIV/AIDS as such or in the mechanics of commercial sex itself. I was thus very pleased to have been able to form good rapport and even friendship with many women once I overcame this stage of first encounter. What is even more satisfying for me was the fact that the cooperation that I got from the women was not materially motivated. I met some women who were extremely poor and would have certainly appreciated financial offers from me, but I was pleased to learn that even these needy women were willing to help in appreciation of what I was trying to do rather than in the hope of getting financial rewards from me. I was also able to identify women with leadership qualities among my first acquaintances and made good use of these women to locate and make acquaintances of other women.

At the end of this phase of my research, which took roughly about a month, I was able to determine whom I should interview intensively, whom I should include in the group interviews, whom I should consult only when I reached the questionnaire-phase and whom I should include in all the three stages. I was also able to get a sense of the morphology of commercial work in the city both in terms of its geographical spread and its various forms. Before starting my work I had hoped to find four "types" of sex workers whose stories, I thought, should constitute the pillars of my study: migrant "prostitutes", non-migrant "prostitutes", "prostitutes" with resident dependents and "prostitutes" with non-resident dependents. My preliminary explorations led me to abandon quickly these hypothetical "types" of sex workers in favor of a more realistic one based on several different variables but principally on the place and conditions of work as well as the place and conditions of residence. I also learnt in this preliminary stage that I stood very little chance of finding part-time or "hidden" sex workers, precisely because these types go by other names rather than as "sex workers". I learnt that whatever pieces of information that I might obtain about them would have to be indirect.

3.1 Individual Interviews

Following this preliminary stage, I undertook extensive interviews with a total of seventeen women whom I selected in part because they represented the various kinds of lives related to commercial work and in part because they were willing and able to tell me about their lives in great detail. In practice, it is the latter criterion that determined the number of interviews that I was able to secure. However much I tried to balance the two criteria, it was not possible to come to a perfect mix of "types" and number of interviews.

Interestingly, however, the randomly obtained distribution of interviews by itself tells a story about commercial sex and the lives of the women behind it. A good number of my intensive interviews came from women who practice the three most common types of commercial sex: sex workers who have rented the house in which they work (but who refer to themselves as "በአልጋ የሚሠሩ", i.e. those who work on beds which they own); sex workers who work in houses and beds owned by others (who refer to themselves as "አካፋይ" (i.e. those who work for share) and street sex workers (who refer to themselves "በአስፋልት ላይ የሚሠሩ" i.e. those who work on the asphalt). Besides being most common in terms of the number of women that engage in them, each of the three forms of commercial sex has other distinctive characteristics of its own. "Work on one's own bed" is distinctive as the most stable of all forms of commercial sex: the women who practice it have been in it continuously for very long spans of time. "Share work" is noted for being unstable because there is a high turnover of the women, but it also happens to be the most common entry point for young women who are recent migrants to the city. "Asphalt work", which contrasts with the two forms of kiosk work because it involves outdoors solicitation, is also the most visible and colorful form of commercial sex work that attracts city girls who grew up in Addis itself.

The details of these characteristics and their significance for the social context of commercial sex will be presented in the book where appropriate. I mention these points here only to explain the slant in the distribution of my one-to-one interviews towards these three forms of commercial sex and to direct attention to the logic that the slant itself carries irrespective of the fact that it was not intentionally created by me. The facts about the distribution of the interviews, however, should not be read to mean that I interviewed women only from two or three categories of sex workers. My informants include women who practice all forms of commercial sex; women who have stayed in commercial sex for long as well as for short periods of time; women who are immigrants as well as native Addis Ababans; women who are educated and women who are illiterate.

Only a few of my interviewees were able to tell me about their lives as *stories*. Most of them patiently answered my various questions in short statements and left the joining of the pieces to me. The very few women who did actually tell me stories of their lives were, however, incredibly good storytellers. All they needed was to be initiated with a general question like "tell me about yourself starting from your childhood". They did not want to be interrupted after that. They determined not only the sequence of the story but also the detail in which they went into each of its parts. The stories were told with such flow, continuity and development that they sounded as though they were rehearsed. These kinds of informants were not only relatively easy to interview but also reduced the workload after the interview: I did not have to worry much about working out the chronology and the interconnections of their lives. The only problem with these storytellers is that they determined everything and focused on selected parts of their lives and were not, consequently, inclined to cover all the areas I wanted them to cover. With some of them these "missed parts" were filled through "negotiations", although with some of the women these negotiations meant that I had to beg for information not voluntarily given.

With those women who gave me information about their lives with one piece of information at a time, I extracted details and verified consistency by posing as many different questions as possible and by posing similar or the same questions in different ways. The interviews were tiresome, and sometimes I had to stop myself for fear that they might degenerate into interrogation. They were nevertheless very good in terms of coverage because I could guide my informants to issues and times in their lives on which I wanted detailed information.

I will use information from intensive interviews to illustrate my major points with very real and concrete examples. I will also use it to involve my informants directly in the description of life behind commercial sex: in short, to let the women speak for themselves.

3.2   Focus Group Discussions

Focus groups were made up of five women for each of the types of sex work currently practiced in the city. For all the seven types of commercial sex work (described below) the women added up to a total of 35 individuals. However, given the sensitivity of research on sex work due to stigma attached to it, it was impossible to go about the selection of the women on the basis of a sampling design prepared in advance. I therefore formed the groups out of the first five women in each category who were willing to participate in the discussions.

I went into focus group discussions with three objectives. One was to get facts about a particular category (or type) of commercial sex workers. These facts are about their average age, education, the average length of time they tended to stay in the work, whether or not they have dependents, etc.   In short, facts that I thought would help me come to some understanding of what the "typical" profile of a sex worker in any given category was. My second objective was to collect information regarding the interaction of women in each category among themselves as well as with other people, individually as well as through membership in institutions such as *idir*, *iqub* and *mahber*. The third objective was to see if there was any kind of "group" awareness and "group" attitude towards people, institutions or conditions (like HIV and AIDS, for instance).

As much as possible I tried to make sure that the women knew each other and were comfortable with each other because I thought that would facilitate my work. I posed the questions to the group, not to individuals. I took care not to dictate who should answer the questions. In fact, as much as possible, I tried to create a discussion atmosphere where the women would freely talk rather than conduct a group interview characterized by question and answer sessions. In all cases, the informants agreed that I tape the conversations rather than take notes on paper. This was very much helpful to let the discussions go freely.

Many of the women who took part in the focus group discussions have been previously interviewed in detail about their own private experiences. I watched as the discussions proceeded for elements of similarity and difference between their personal stories and the overall story of the group to which they belonged. I noticed very few differences. The differences that did exist were explainable in terms of the age of the women or the length of time they had worked.

The whole effort in the focus group discussions was to have the women talk as representatives of a "group" or "category", talking as "we" rather than as "I". However, many times I had to allow the speakers to talk about them or about other individuals as examples of characteristics or conditions they shared with others in the group. I also took note of the points on which the women agreed and those points on which they disagreed. In both cases I took note of the degree of agreement and of disagreement.

I tried to have the discussions proceed in the order that I set out in my preliminary list of questions. However, in almost all cases that did not work. The women answered some of the questions before I asked them and the discussions made some of the questions irrelevant or unnecessary.

I used information obtained from focus group discussions in two ways: as direct evidence for group characteristics, as pointed out above, and as input for the questionnaire that I formulated to get information from a larger number of women. The questionnaire was finally administered to all women, including those that I have intensively interviewed and those that have participated in the focus group discussions.

3.3   Direct Observation

My observation of the women's social life involved their interactions with family members (where these existed) neighbors and friends. What is interesting about this aspect of my research is that I never planned for an "observation session", and did not take or make time for it. It just happened simultaneously with my work with individual interviewees or with my work with the focus groups. In the middle of an interview a neighbor walks in, asks for something or simply settles herself in; or a friend is invited for a coffee with a guest (that is me!); there were also very many, long or short "time outs" during the interviews during which a family member, a neighbor or some other guest is attended to or accommodated in a relaxed situation. There were a couple of times when the formal interviews were rescheduled because some important person had arrived and we allowed life to take its normal course between my informants and their visitors. A great deal of information was collected about socialization among sex workers as well as between them and others during these unintended and unscheduled breaks.

Similar things happened during focus group discussions. Typically the discussions took place in the house of one of the women and involved friends, neighbors or acquaintances. Even if all members of a focus group were not close friends, there were always some that were. In fact, it was the women themselves who suggested to me who the members of each group should be, and I disagreed with their suggestions only in rare cases. Typically, the setting of the focus group discussion was the kind of setting that the women were familiar with almost on a daily basis, involving the partaking of coffee or the chewing of *chat* in a relaxed and casual home atmosphere. A great deal of material not expected in the focus group discussions came my way simply as the women interacted with each other and talked freely.

In at least two instances, I was able to observe women who are friends of each other and who worked together in work place settings. This involved only the women who worked in the bars and hotels. No formal interviews were scheduled and there was no awareness among the subjects that I came to observe them at work. I went simply by way of dropping in to say hello. In both cases the establishments were drinking places where I could theoretically come as a customer. These observations yielded valuable information on the emotional and material contents of the relationships among sex workers as well as between the women and a range of other people.

3.4 Questionnaire-based Sample Survey

In this final stage of my research I collected quantitative data by collecting responses to a prepared questionnaire. This information came from a pool of 100 women who work as commercial sex workers.

3.4.1   Target population

The population targeted for surveying consisted of all female sex workers in Addis Ababa who are full time practitioners and who openly acknowledge their engagement in the practice. This meant that clandestine operators or part-time operators were not included.

3.4.2   Sample size

The actual number of women engaged in sex work in Addis Ababa is anybody's guess. Statistics on this are highly impressionistic and imprecise. I found it therefore both impossible and inaccurate to try to decide on a sample size on the basis of some hypothetical figure about the target population.   I decided to work with a sample size of 100 respondents basically on the basis of resources and time available to me for this research.

3.4.3   Sampling method

The nature of the topic precluded a relatively simpler method of stratified random sampling for the selection of all the respondents. Due to the stigma associated with commercial sex, it was impossible to expect that sex workers selected at random on the basis of a neat stratified scheme would cooperate as respondents. I also decided not to use strict random sampling because that would have predetermined the distribution of respondents within each stratum. This would have been a mistake because my project partly was to get a sense of the distribution of sex workers of Addis Ababa among the different types of sex work.

The questionnaire survey was therefore based on a sampling method that consisted of two variables that were nevertheless employed independently of each other to select respondents. The first variable was geographical distribution and the second was types of sex work. I am aware of the fact that commercial sex work is diffuse in Addis Ababa and it will be misleading to talk about any locality in the city that is totally free from the practice. It is nonetheless true that there are specific parts of the city in which there are concentrated settlements of sex workers (See details on this in chapter 4). I selected seven localities that are fairly widely recognized as centers of commercial sex in Addis Ababa. These were Mercato, Piazza, Arat Kilo, Casanchis, Cherqos, Meshwualekia and Kolfe. I decided that each of these localities should be represented in my sample by a minimum of 5 individuals who either live in these localities or practice sex work in these localities.

I was, however, aware of the fact that there were a significant number of sex workers who neither lived nor worked in these major centers. Therefore, I decided to include them in the sample through the second variable, i.e. type of sex work. I identified seven distinct types of sex work in Addis Ababa on the basis of information from the one-to-one interviews and focus group discussions. These were fixed-share workers, equal-share workers, independent home-based operators, streetwalkers, hotel and night club sex workers, bar sex workers, and sex workers operating out of small drinking places (see chapter 3 for details).

I decided, likewise, that each of the types should be represented in my sample by at least 5 individuals. That the number of localities and types of sex work was equal is purely a coincidence, not designed. How many individuals would actually come from each of the localities and how many of the individuals will actually represent each type of sex work in the overall sample of 100 individuals was not, therefore, determined in advance. The sample was controlled to ensure the representation of each locality and each type of sex work for a minimum of 20% of the total sample in each case.

My strategy was to recruit individuals from among the women with whom I had already worked in the context of the one-to-one interviews and the focus group discussions to help me with the location and persuasion of respondents for the questionnaire survey. This recruitment of coordinators was based on their association with either a locality or with a type of sex work or both. However, I did not leave the task of locating respondents to the coordinators. I was careful not to end up with a distorted distribution due to the unequal diligence of the coordinators.

As it turned out, the final list of respondents reflected what I believe to be a representative sample of female-sex workers in Addis Ababa. The representation of the localities as well as the types of work was unequal. For the localities, the representation turned out to be as follows: 14 came from Merkato, 14 from Piazza, 8 each from Cherqos and Arat Kilo, 9 from Kolfe and a striking 41 came from Meshualekia. Only six other individuals came from outside of the localities in my list.

For the types of sex work the distribution was as follows: 5 individuals (the minimal number) were from small drinking places; another 5 were equal-share operators; 7 were women who operated from bars; 12 were independent home-based operators; 25 were streetwalkers; 35, the largest number, were fixed-rate share operators and 11 were sex workers based in Hotels and nightclubs.

That there is sometimes no correlation, or even closeness, between the two distributions should not be surprising. That is because there is a degree to which some localities tend to specialize in one or another type of sex work so that there may be no individuals in some localities to represent some of the types of sex work.

3.4.4   Questionnaire design and administration

The questionnaire turned out to be somewhat lengthy because it sought to accommodate as many of the categories and conditions of commercial sex work as possible and cover all the areas and issues for which I wanted answers. However, most questions included in the response section a "non-applicable (NA)" category in the knowledge that they may apply to some categories of women and not to others. This made a single questionnaire more efficient than separate questionnaires for the different categories of women.

I administered and filled out the questionnaire in person. This was helpful in terms of the accuracy of communication with the women. Despite the length of the questionnaire the interview period for each respondent was relatively short. This was partly because, as I have pointed out above, the women whom I have selected as coordinators helped in preparing the women for the sessions. Partly it was because, once I identified the type of sex work that a respondent engages in, I could quickly move through the questionnaire by asking only the relevant questions.

There is practically no aspect of the lives of women in commercial sex that the questionnaire did not touch upon. Most of this information has been processed into quantitative data. However, some of it, often collected in response to unspecified choices or categories in the questionnaire under the category "other(s)", has netted valuable qualitative material. The information from the questionnaire survey was deployed in my discussion of classification of sex workers as well as their social behaviors and makes a significant component of chapters 3 to 5.

4   General Observations on "Fieldwork" among sex workers

Maybe because I grew up in Addis Ababa and went to school in the Markato area (close to one of the major centers of commercial sex work), or because I had some experience working with sex workers when I did my BA thesis, the idea of doing research that involves contacting and talking to women who are in this line of work did not sound too difficult for me at first. I was used to seeing women standing in front of the bars and small drinking houses along the main streets through which I passed to go to school in the early 1990s. The idea had never crossed my mind that these were dangerous women. The three women whose life stories I wrote for a History BA thesis (Bethlehem, 2000, 2002) had welcomed me when I approached them for interviews and struck me with their disarming honesty. In retrospect, these were probably the reasons for which I thought of doing work that might focus on the *humanity* of these women and why, when I framed my proposal for this study, I was not gearing up to do work among a "dangerous" or "vicious" group of people.

It is, therefore, very remarkable that more than once at the very beginning of the research I momentarily thought that I might have been wrong about all of this. That was because of the immediate reactions of many people, both men and women, with whom I shared the topic of the research that I was going to begin. Many felt that I was courting danger; others advised that I should be extremely careful because I could be robbed or beaten up by the women. Almost all, with the exception of some of my closest friends, thought that this was a very difficult thing to do particularly for a woman like me because the women would not take kindly on a woman coming from a high place like a university and talking down to them. These are brutalized women, many said to me, and they are very unpredictable. A daily dose of these warning statements must have had an impact on me, for on my diary for November 4, 2003, I wrote:

> I lose hope sometimes about this whole thing. I am beginning to curse the day I decided to do research on this topic…What has put the most pressure on me is the attitude of the public towards the work…Many people are telling me to be careful because

there are many ways in which HIV is transmitted from one person to the other! Others are saying that it will be difficult for me not to be mistaken by men for a prostitute! Still others expressed worry that I surely will need a lot of money to entertain all these women to be able to talk to them…

In retrospect, however, I realize that my frustration came from my uncertainty as to where to begin and how to get in touch with the women. For I thought that if I made the wrong start and began with the really "bad variety" of women I might fail disastrously. I was also afraid that I might be misunderstood by the women or rejected out of hand. However, once I made the contacts through friends and an NGO that worked among sex workers, I was quickly reassured about the validity of my earlier thoughts about the women. I have to admit, however, that I have at the beginning listened a little too much to what I would call "prostitute-bashing". I nearly succumbed to the very thing that I was going out to study and refute: the idea that "prostitutes" *by definition* are dangerous and criminal elements.

As I had expected and hoped, I was able to strike out a friendship with many of the women I was introduced to. I did not find their company threatening or in any way unnatural. In fact, it was very easy for me to forget sometimes that I was spending time in surroundings that people consider dangerous or in the company of "vicious" women. I did not feel insecure or unsafe even among the mostly young sex workers who work in the streets and who candidly told me that they *do* sometimes help themselves to the pockets of drunken men.

This brings me to the question of trust and the feelings of the women about my representations of them. As I pointed out above, the difficulty I had with the women was in convincing them that I was interested in their lives rather than in what they could tell me about how we can protect society from them. At first everybody's immediate assumption was that I was going to ask questions about HIV. And the reaction was rather negative and dismissive. One of the women who later ended up being my chief coordinator and organizer said to me, for instance, that "…you people think that it is us who transmit AIDS to people. We have told many people who asked us about this that may be they should go to the schools and talk to the schoolgirls about it or to the secretaries in the offices; there is nothing different that we will be telling you." Another said that she "…did not know what people did with all the responses they have collected from us before… I did not see anything coming out of it for us".

Patient explanation and down-to-earth statements of what I was looking for always converted the women from doubters to enthusiastic supporters. It was not difficult for most of them to understand what academic research meant. I did not present myself as somebody who comes from some agency or institution whose decisions can affect their lives. I told them that I was a student and that I needed their help. Only one woman, among over a hundred that I talked to, said that she has something better to do with her time. In short, the women had no illusions about the purpose of the study and cooperated willingly. Consequently they expressed no worry or doubt about how they might be represented in my work.

With most of the women, particularly those that I interviewed in detail for their personal stories, the interviews were very candid and straightforward. There was nothing that was off limits. In fact, in many cases it was the women themselves who took over the lead in the conversation and who therefore not only pre-empted the questions that I wanted to pose to them but even talked about the things that I would have hesitated to ask because of ethical considerations. The only point on which I felt uncomfortable asking questions was on how much the women charge for the services they give to clients. I took note when this information is freely given, but did not pursue it. For my purposes it was enough to obtain general information on the economic or financial conditions of the women.

I have stated above that most of my informants, particularly those who took part in the one-to-one interviews and the focus group discussions were very friendly towards me; what that friendliness included was that there was very little that they wanted to hide from me about their identity. Only one woman asked me to hide her name in what I was going to write. Most did not, although almost all said it would be a good idea if I referred to them only by their given names rather than by their full names. The idea is that female names like Almaz, Yeshi, Tigist, Zerfe, or Fantu are so common that they would not raise eyebrows, even if a relative or kin were to run into them in my work. The woman who asked me to hide her identity said so because she had a sibling right then studying at Addis Ababa University.

In short, I have learnt in the course of this research that scholarly work among sex workers in Addis Ababa is relatively easy for a female researcher with empathy, once the line is crossed and the contact is made with them. I say relatively easy because I have the feeling that it would not have been as easy for male researchers. The women were able to talk to me with a kind of freedom and candidness that I did not expect at all at the beginning. Many of them were quite explicit about their vocation, and told me everything about their lives, and even, as I said, about things that I did not ask about. Of course, many times I broke down and cried when I heard some of their heart-rending stories; most of the time I was deeply touched, but invariably I was sad about the suffering that they were all undergoing. I don't know if this sense of empathy came from the fact of my being female also; maybe. But I simply do not think that their hearts and their mouths would have opened as easily for a male researcher.

5   Scope and Limitations of the Study

The framework in which this study was conceived and carried out was based on the premise that an exploration of the social context of "prostitution" should involve both an intensive examination of the various forms of "the social" and an extensive enough coverage to ensure that the data are representative. The social context in this work is taken broadly to include two elements: *social ties* that exist between sex workers and various other individuals and groups of people and *social transactions* as combinations of obligations and benefits that come with the ties. Through this broad exploration of the social arena in this study I hope to contribute to our knowledge about commercial sex in Ethiopia in two important ways: first by taking the inquiry to an area that has been neglected so far, second by undertaking that inquiry in some detail. In short, this study deals with a relatively new set of issues within an otherwise familiar topic of commercial sex and deals with these issues in some detail. As such, it both extends and deepens the scope of our knowledge about the topic.

Since this research is done in Addis Ababa only, its conclusions, strictly speaking, apply to contemporary Addis Ababa alone. However, there are many reasons why the material from Addis Ababa could be taken to be illustrative of conditions and processes in other parts of urban Ethiopia (with some significant exceptions, of course). First of all, Addis Ababa is both the capital and the biggest urban center in Ethiopia.

Ethiopian society is represented in the city both in its mixed and differentiated forms. With some exaggeration, the city and its social morphology could be taken as Ethiopia in miniature. Secondly, well over half of the women who practice commercial sex are migrants to the city (although, unlike previous times, these do not constitute an absolute majority anymore). As such, not only do they relate their experiences to developments in virtually all parts of Ethiopia, but also most of them maintain social ties and connections with the regions and localities from which they had come. There is, therefore, a lot of information about other parts of the country in the stories of Addis Ababa's sex workers. A significant number of the women had also worked as sex workers in other towns and cities of Ethiopia, some going back and forth between Addis and these cities and towns. The experiences in Addis Ababa and other urban settlements are therefore not only similar but also frequently directly interconnected.

This is a study of the social universe of women who practice commercial sex *openly*. Its findings relate directly to the experiences of women who are avowed sex workers. Because of this, it has a number of limitations as a study of the social context of commercial sex *in general*. One of the limitations lies in the fact that a great deal of commercial sex occurs underground, referred to in the literature (rather inaccurately) as part-time sex work. Women who might engage in commercial sex work might describe themselves not only as bartenders or as waitresses in bars and pastry shops but also as sales girls, office workers or students. In fact, what makes it very difficult to gauge the prevalence of commercial sex as a whole is the difficulty of gauging this underground component. The social stigma that attaches to commercial sex work makes it almost impossible to contact or talk to the practitioners in this category.

The general belief is that underground sex work is widespread in Addis Ababa, but it is very difficult to come up even with an estimate. This puts a sort of structural limitation to the kind of study that I undertake here. It is difficult for me to resist the feeling that what I might manage to tell, at best, is only half the story. The only strategy I could find to reduce the absolute sense of helplessness that I felt about this matter was to seek information about underground sex workers from those who operate openly. It is also noteworthy that many women who openly practice in some parts of the town are not known as such in other parts of the town. To a certain extent, therefore, the open practitioner and the hidden practitioner might be one and the same.

There are other limitations also. Despite my claim that this is a study of the social context of commercial sex in Addis Ababa, this study does not include the perspectives of a range of people and interests with whom the women in commercial sex come into daily contact. It does not, therefore, compare and contrast what the women had to say with what their children, parents, relatives, neighbors, landlords, pimps, bar owners, lovers or clients might say about them. In other words, in this study the social universe surrounding commercial sex is depicted through the eyes of the women themselves. Nor does the study breakdown or differentiate the groups, interests and institutions that are often collectively referred to as "the public" or "society". Elements of the public or society who have involved themselves in the matter of commercial sex and in the lives of the women who practice it range from law makers to government ministries and the police, from neighborhood administrations (the *qabales*), to *idirs* and NGOs. The ways in which each of these units has been involved in the work and the lives of sex workers and the assumptions or premises that have guided their actions is not part of the story in this work.

I recognize the above two limitations as significant limitations of the study. They arose partly from the fact that the study is a student project conducted with limited resources in a limited time frame. Partly they arose from the women-centered approach that I have chosen, as described above. Yet, I recognize that the social context of commercial sex in Addis Ababa will not be complete until it has combined all these missing perspectives with the perspectives of the women. I hope to be able to do this in the future in another context.

6 "Prostitutes" vs. "Sex Workers": What is in a name?

At this early stage, I think it is necessary and useful to explain my choice of the term "sex worker(s)" over the more common term "prostitute(s)" and, by implication, the term "sex work" over "prostitution". I find it necessary to explain this choice not only because I anticipate that my readers might ask this question but also because the choice was also a hard one for me to make and I still maintain a degree of ambivalence about both sets of terms. This ambivalence will also be reflected both in my perspectives on existing literature and in my interpretation of my own research findings.

As I will show in some detail in the following chapter, the term "prostitute" has come to carry moralistic connotations. It has for long been employed to separate sex workers from other women, among other things, in terms of their supposed differences on sexual morality. The term evokes the image of the shameless, loose and corrupt woman who has chosen to live a public life of promiscuity in full defiance of social morality. By "prostituting" herself, the woman has made a choice to "market her flesh" and service her own lust or the lust of unknown men. To refer to the women as "prostitutes" would thus carry the implication that I also agree with this common and highly moralistic interpretation. I do not. That is simply because I do not believe that women in commercial sex choose to be in the situation they find themselves in.

Equally difficult for me to accept is the implication that would follow the use of the term "prostitute" in its noun form. "Prostitution", in common use, refers simply to what the "prostitute" does: the provision of sexual services commercially, be it by choice or otherwise. Only sometimes does this common use include what the employers of the women (like bar and night-club owners, madams, pimps or other sex capitalists) do. However, I find this use to be deeply mistaken. "Prostitution", I believe, is an institution that should be understood comprehensively "as a set of social relations which involves the provider of sexual services [and two other categories of people], *the receivers or buyers* [of sex] *and the regulator* [of the whole business]" (Emphasis added; Truong, 1990:15). Referring as "prostitution" only to the part played by the women without including the part played by the purchasers of sex and by the state or its agencies that regulate, tax, proscribe or indirectly take part in the business (like the tourism industry for instance), would be, I think, both inaccurate and unfair. If there are moral consequences to what is done in "prostitution", then the consequences should be shared by all those who are involved in it, persons as well as institutions. In light of this, I thought that "sex work" might be a less loaded and hypocritical a term than "prostitution". The phrase "sex work" has also an added advantage of presenting the part of the women in "prostitution" as labor. Sex work, indeed, is labor, a hard and painful form of labor at that. This, at least, is what almost all of my 117 informants have stated categorically.

This is not to say that "sex worker" and "sex work" are non-problematic designations. As with "prostitute" and "prostitution", the problem with these terms derives in part from the way they have been put to use by those who first coined and popularized them. The terms were coined and popularized by liberal feminist groups who sought to present "sex work" as a line of work freely chosen by adult women whose rights as workers should be respected and whose control over their sexuality should not be interfered with by the state (Rosenblum, 1975; Jaggar, 1983). While this perspective is powerful as a negation of the hypocrisy implied in the use of "prostitute" and "prostitution", it implies a justification of sex work that ignores the simple facts of dehumanization and exploitation involved in it. "This is not work" said one of my female informants, "it is a work you would not want to call work but for lack of any other term" (Shewaye). Another one refers to sex work as "work [in which one plays] with fire…a kind of work in which you wouldn't tell people who you are" (Tirusew). The assertion that sex work is like work in the office or in the factory is a proposition that is very difficult for me to accept. There is something unique and different about converting one's body into a commodity. That is why I feel a bad aftertaste every time I use the expression "sex work". Yet, I believe that bad aftertaste is infinitely better than feeling hypocritical or unfair. Thus I would use "sex work" and "sex workers", rather than "prostitution" and "prostitutes". I will use the latter combination of terms only in referring to previous uses critically or when I cite or quote previous writers, always in inverted commas.

7   Organization of the book

This book is divided into 6 chapters. Chapter 2 surveys the literature on commercial sex with a particular focus on the shifting images and approaches of the female sex worker in Western, African and Ethiopian societies across time. The chapter presents the diverse approaches to sex work and sex workers across cultures and times but establishes the essential point that in all views "prostitutes" are collectively represented either as "debased" or as "exploited" categories of women.   Chapter 3 will present a scheme for the differentiation of the sex worker population of Addis Ababa and accounts for significant changes that have occurred in the demographic characteristics and mode of operation of sex workers in the city since the 1970s and 1980s. Chapter 4 will utilize the scheme outlined in chapter 4 and actually identify and describe the various categories in Addis Ababa. Chapter 5 will tackle the issue of how sex workers relate to non-sex workers, be they family, kin, friends, clients, neighbors, men or women. It will describe the efforts that the women make to stay "normal" and to remain decent human beings. Chapter 6 concludes the work by presenting the main arguments of the study and insights gained in the course of the study.

Chapter Two

Western, African and Ethiopian Images and Approaches to Female Sex Workers

In this chapter I will try to highlight some of the major positions and views in the literature concerning commercial sex workers. I will do this by breaking down the material into three sections under which I will discuss Western, African and Ethiopian themes and approaches. This breakdown is justified in part because it reflects the cultural and historical elements to which I want to call attention in this study. It is also useful because it enables me to proceed from the general to the specific as the literature on commercial sex in Africa (and therefore in Ethiopia) has been considerably influenced by Western paradigms and views. I recognize that making a distinction between Africa and Ethiopia in any kind of scholarly endeavor is both overdrawn and dangerous. It is overdrawn because Ethiopian realities are not in the main different from realities in the rest of Africa. It is dangerous because this kind of approach feeds into the problem of Ethiopian exceptionalism, a serious problem in which Ethiopian studies finds itself and owing to which it suffers from some degree of intellectual isolation. Despite this caveats, however, I will break down the review into "African" and "Ethiopian" not only because the remainder of this work will be specifically on Ethiopia but also because the literature on the rest of Africa is scanty and mostly inaccessible to me while, in contrast, I am close to the vast but mostly unpublished material on Ethiopia.

I will make one major argument in this chapter: that existing literature does not provide adequate and satisfactory answers to the most contested issue in the whole matter of commercial sex, namely, the difference between those women who practice it and those who do not practice it. That is because no one appears to have been interested in the social life of the sex workers beyond their work of selling sex. In place of a cultural and historically sensitive study of sex workers as social beings what we have is what one writer (Truong, 1990) calls "homogenizing" the women in either of two ways. One way of "homogenizing" the women separates them collectively from all other women, and puts them in a category by themselves, doing so only on the basis of their vocation. It thus imposes upon them an identity as a group and associates each individual woman with personality traits supposedly shared by all sex workers. The other way of "homogenizing" the women lumps or combines them with all other women and denies or underplays the specificity of their work and what this kind of work means for their lives. This approach takes the work or condition of sex workers as just another form of oppression and exploitation in which all women find themselves under patriarchal orders.

The first way of homogenizing sex workers has implications for how the women are conceived as a social group and as individuals because it associates the work with personality traits. The second way of homogenizing sex workers, on the other hand, simply proceeds from *denying* the validity of the first way of homogenizing them and goes into its own job of homogenizing the women with all other women; it does not find it necessary to show *how* the first way of homogenizing was incorrect.

My position throughout this book is that neither of these extreme forms of "homogenizing" sex workers is fully correct. Women who practice commercial sex should not be lumped together and labeled, as one would label a factory product that is made out of basically the same raw material. Such labels for sex workers have almost always involved value judgments as to the character and social worth of the women. Nor should sex workers be fused indistinctly into a rather too broad category of "oppressed women" because what sex workers do to earn money, in my belief, is both specific in its nature and significant in terms of its impact on their lives. It is in this framework that, after a survey of the literature, I will put forward a thesis for a differentiated analysis of female sex workers in Addis Ababa.

1 Western Images and Approaches: From the Upper Class Courtesan to the Worker-Whore

It is frequently stated that the typical Western view of commercial sex and sex workers, as reflected in public or academic literature, evolved from Christian moral principles that define promiscuity as a sin. The "prostitute", according to this notion, is taken primarily as a sinner by virtue of engaging in promiscuous sex. It is further said that, despite sharing this common element, European thinkers, writers and decision makers have forwarded different ideas about what should be done with the "sin" and the "sinners". Some argued that the sinners should be separated from the sin, and as much as possible, salvaged. Others argued that the sinners are inseparable from the sin, suggesting that sex workers should be prosecuted and forced to abandon their trade in the interest of public well-being. It is these two notions that are said to have been behind the opposing camps traditionally referred to as "the regulation school" and "the abolition school".

In actual fact, however, Western perceptions and perspectives on commercial sex were much more complex. They cannot be simply reduced to different interpretations of Christian sexual morality. In terms of time also, some of the themes and views about commercial sex predate the emergence of Christianity while others are as recent as the nineteenth and twentieth centuries.

With some risk of overgeneralization, we can talk in terms of two broad forms of discourse with regard to commercial sex in Western Europe. One of them is what we might call a male-centered discourse, focusing on the interests of what it regarded as "normal" society rather than on the interests of the women who practiced commercial sex. The principal issues that this discourse tries to address are issues such as public morality, public health and public safety. The other form of discourse is what we might call a female-centered discourse, seeking to focus on the interests and perspectives of the women. The issue on which this discourse has focused is gender inequality in politics, the economy and society, and the meaning of this inequality both for the recruitment of women for sex work and for the way they live in it. The first form of discourse is obviously the oldest form, and the more influential of the two. The second form was relatively very recent and is somewhat still marginal.

1.1 From the Fallen Woman to the Dirty Whore: "Patriarchy" and Western Images of the Sex Worker

The male-centered or patriarchal[1] discourse on commercial sex in the West almost always began with what we might call the *de-linking* of the woman who becomes a "prostitute" from normal or mainstream society,

---

[1] I will refer to this discourse as patriarchal discourse without necessarily subscribing to the views of those who gave it this name.

and then proceeded to *re-link* her to that society with a new identity and with supposedly new behavior and attitude. In pre-Christian times, this *de-linking* simply meant that the "prostitute" was viewed primarily as a woman who has dissociated herself from family or kin or as a person who had been lost to her folks either due to rebellion or due to the intervention of some extraordinary force. Moreover, the *de-linking* might or might not have involved the physical movement of the woman away from her place of birth or upbringing. What it meant was that once the break from "normal" society had taken place the woman's conduct as regards sex was not be governed by rules applying to the rest of the society. It is also noteworthy that in pre-Christian times this dissociation from normal society was not necessarily regarded as a tragedy for the woman. In Greek society, for instance, the "prostitute" could enjoy a high status and command respect, depending on the social class and status of the men to whom she provides sexual services. "Prostitution" could also be associated with religious rites and rituals, so that becoming a "prostitute" could be regarded as a "calling" over which the woman had little or no control.

Similarly, in pre-Christian Europe the *re-linking* of the "prostitute" with society did not necessarily involve redefinition of the woman as an immoral and dangerous person, although this redefinition did exist in certain cultures and communities. Again, depending on the class to which it is provided as a service, or depending on whether or not it is associated with some religious ritual, commercial sex could be regarded as a badge of honor rather than of disgrace and dishonor.

It is with the triumph of Christianity that promiscuity came to be publicly regarded as sin, and the promiscuous woman became, first and foremost, a sinner. Moreover, according to Christians, the woman who broke off from normal society to become a "prostitute" had not only undergone a personal tragedy of alienation but had also dishonored and cheapened herself. However, there is one element that is very interesting and noteworthy about the views of early Christians regarding commercial sex workers. This element is that Christians did not proceed from their idea of the sinful or the fallen woman to the idea of a bad woman who poses danger to society. In other words, for most of its history Christianity did not *re-link* the "prostitute" to society in adversarial terms. The positions taken by Saint Augustine and Saint Thomas Aquinas, for instance, reflect the attitude of Christians during the medieval period on this issue. Both saints condemned commercial sex, but wrote that it is a useful (if not a necessary) evil. Saint Augustine's view was that if "prostitution" were to be abolished "you will pollute all things with lust"; for this reason, therefore, the practice is "a lawful immorality". "Take away the sewage", Saint Thomas Aquinas wrote on his part, "and you will fill the place with pollution…take away the prostitutes from the world and you will fill it with sodomy" (Quoted in Parrinder, 1980: 225-6). In short, the position of early Christians was that "prostitution" was necessary because it caters to male lust that is somehow natural and that, by doing so, it will help protect society. Commercial sex was also tolerated in Medieval Europe in part because it was fiscally useful. Governments or potentates collected taxes from brothels (Chauvin, cited in Truong, 1990).

The conversion of the promiscuous and, therefore, the sinful woman, to the dangerous woman who debases not just herself but also society was a process that took a long period of time to be completed in Western Europe. It was a process punctuated by significant historical developments, some of them socio-cultural, some of them socio-economic. In the first category, for instance, one can mention two important phenomena: the development of religious purism that started with Protestantism in the sixteenth century and the development of the social purism that became characteristic of the so-called Victorian age during the nineteenth century. The first form of purism advocated personal discipline and moral rectitude while the second form proclaimed the advent of "civilized" society. These different forms of purism developed rather far apart from each other in terms of time. They also affected different parts of Europe unequally, at least at the beginning. Moreover, they developed first among small sections of society, usually among those that regarded themselves as "the chosen" or as elite types. However, the movements later spread throughout the continent, going beyond their geographical or social points of origin. Eventually, they created a social atmosphere characterized by high level of intolerance, regimentation and self-righteousness.

These culturally significant developments took place at the same time as significant changes were taking place in the social structure of West European society triggered by urbanization and industrialization. Both of these phenomena were attended by widespread social dislocation caused by the destruction of old patterns of life associated with the countryside. In many cases they brought about the abolition of social units and institutions with which people were familiar before; in some cases, they dictated the reconstitution of the social units and institutions along new lines. The result was the emergence of large masses of people, men and women, for whom the new environment was strange, unfamiliar, alienating and stressful. One result of this was the expansion of commercial sex both as a source of livelihood for women who had limited sources of self-sustenance in the new environment and as a service catering to the sexual needs of a large male population of workers. Commercial sex was also associated with alcohol, the two of them becoming frequent pastimes of the working class in the industrial towns and cities (Tobias, 1972).

It is important to note that the framework within which commercial sex is discussed in Western Europe ever since the nineteenth century is determined by the interrelationship between the two phenomena I have just described: the socio-cultural phenomenon of purism, characterized by the hardening of the language towards commercial sex and the women who practiced it, and the socio-economic phenomenon of urbanization, poverty and alienation that made "prostitution" a lower class affair. The hardening of the language itself was a reflection of the fact that the former upper class "prostitute", the so-called "courtesan", had become socially extinct, leaving the field to the "prostitute" of lower class origin. It is not surprising that the upper class, which dominated the discourse, started to define the work of the lower class "prostitute" as a typical embodiment of immorality and crime.

An additional element that accompanied the shift of the language about the "prostitute" from the fallen woman to the immoral and criminal woman was the appearance and spread of sexually transmitted diseases in Europe. One of these diseases was syphilis. The disease, which transatlantic travelers in the 15th century are believed to have introduced to Europe, became a major public health concern in the sixteenth century. It continued to be so all the way to the beginning of the twentieth century when the bacterial agent that causes it was discovered and a cure was developed. In the meantime, widespread fear of the disease meant that women who engaged in promiscuous sex came to be regarded as major public health hazards. The language about the "prostitute" thus came to include in its vocabulary terms that carry connotations of "contamination" and "disease".

By the nineteenth century, therefore, the typical "prostitute" in Western Europe had come to be characterized by two attributes: a socially dead or alienated person who did not have kin or community that she calls her own (Paterson, 1982), and a person who is a major liability to society, embodying and symbolizing immorality, crime and disease.

1.2 From the Victim of Sexual Violence to the Sexual Entrepreneur: The Women's Movement and Western Images of the Sex Worker

The counter-arguments to the male-centered form of discourse on commercial sex and sex workers came rather late in time. They came along with the Women's Movement in the twentieth century, which actually picked up momentum only from the latter part of the 1960s onwards. For about half a century now, writings containing these counter-arguments have accumulated, building into a voluminous literature that has several versions and different areas of emphasis.

Three principal strands of argument can be discerned in the female-centered discourse on commercial sex, each of which is associated with a particular characterization of the women who practice it. The first argument is made by feminist writers who describe commercial sex work as a form of domination of women by men through control over their sexuality. Their argument is associated with characterizations of sex workers as *victims* of this domination. The second argument is made by Liberal feminists who describe commercial sex work as an occupational choice by women who face discrimination in the job market. This argument is associated with characterization of sex workers as *sexual entrepreneurs*. The third argument is made by Marxist-influenced feminist writers who describe "prostitution" as an effort to survive by commercializing an aspect of domestic reproductive work for which capital, the state or society have refused to pay or pay very little. This argument is associated with characterizations of sex workers as *poor women* who are trying to survive by taking to the market that which is "most theirs".

The most vocal and highly political response to the male-centered discourse has come from feminist writers and activists for whom "prostitution" is a form of control and abuse of female sexuality by men. According to this group, male control over female sexuality is made possible by the construction of gender and gender roles by patriarchal ideology. In the words of C. McKinnon, this patriarchal ideology is not about economic or other forms of power; it is about power over women through the subjugation of their sexuality. She writes:

> [It is about] the male pursuit of and control over female sexuality…men not as individuals or as biological beings, but as a gender group characterized by maleness as socially constructed, of which this pursuit is definitive…rape in marriage expresses the male sense of entitlement to access to the women they annex, incest extends it…pornography becomes difficult to distinguish from art and ads since it is clear that what is degrading to women is compelling to the consumer. Prostitutes sell [what] pornography advertises… rape, incest, sexual harassment, pornography and prostitution are not primarily abuse of physical force, violence, authority or economics. They are abuse of sex. They need not and do not rely for their coerciveness upon forms of enforcement other than sexual (MacKinon, 1982, cited in Truong, 1990: 45-46).

With regard to commercial sex, there are two strands of argument that follow from this position of Feminists who engage in sexual politics. The first is, as stated above, that "prostitution" is a form of sexual violence against women, albeit one among many other forms of abuse. The second is that "prostitution" should be blamed not on the women but on those men who purchase sex or on those who make profits from it, like pimps and procurers (Barry, 1981a; 1981b). There is no doubt where this group of Feminists stands with regard to the "regulation" vs. "abolition" debate regarding commercial sex work. It is firmly in support of the abolition school, arguing that to condone "prostitution" is to condone the mistreatment and abuse of women.

More directly relevant to the concerns of this study is what Feminists in this category have to say about the women who practice commercial sex. "Prostitutes", they argue, are *victims* of one of the worst forms of sexual domination; they are women from whom the very essence of womanhood has been wrenched away by the dominant male establishment. This is true, they further argue, whether or not the victims realize or accept their condition. In fact, Feminists in this category do not give much consideration to the views or opinions of female sex workers, partly because they suspect that the latter may have a kind of "false consciousness" about their condition. They suspect that patriarchal ideology that was at the very core of the problem might have gone into the heads of its victims. Therefore the "prostitute" comes out not only as a victim of male sexual domination but also as victim of male ideological domination (de Beauvoir, 1974; Chodorow, 1978). The worst-case scenario is that this viewpoint could make the victims somehow part of the problem also, and might condone the manhandling of the "prostitutes" in the process of curbing "prostitution", like throwing the baby out along with the bathwater. This strand of Feminism shares little by way of common interest or agenda with the international sex workers movement (Barry, 1984).

The second strand of Feminist argument portrays "prostitution" as an alternative means of income that women are forced to resort to in a highly discriminatory labor market. This category of writers argue that "prostitution" is a pre-eminently economic, not a political, institution. If there is any politics at all behind it, it is in the abstract sense of male domination showing itself in the job market heavily slanted in favor of men. Under circumstances in which the distribution of jobs is pervaded by male bias, and women are denied opportunities for decent employment, the argument goes; it is not surprising that the victims of discrimination turn to an area in which they have a natural "comparative advantage" over the men (Rosenblum 1975; Heyl, 1979; McLeod, 1982).

This strand of Feminism is unique for its stand on the "regulation-abolition" debate. It declares itself totally opposed to both regulation and abolition because it regards both positions as implying that there is something criminal about commercial sex work. To arrive at this conclusion, Liberal Feminism subscribes to the idea of consensual sex as something personal and private, as something over which the state or any public authority has no rights to legislate or otherwise intervene (Jaggar, 1983).

With regard to the women who practice commercial sex, Liberal Feminism is unique in giving them the exalted title of "entrepreneurs". It argues that what "prostitutes" do is really in no way different from what non-prostitute or married women do. They say that both categories of women employ the same means (i.e. granting sexual favors) towards the same end (i.e. material gain); the only difference is that the "prostitute" has chosen to make the most of it by taking her ware to the open market (Rosenblum, 1975; Heyl, 1979; McLeod, 1982). This characterization of the sex worker as a businesswoman is consistent with the overall goal of Liberal Feminist agenda. That agenda asserts that "prostitutes" should not be denied the human rights and the protection of the law that are advocated for other categories of people; that, in fact, the law should curb not the activities of the real sex workers but those of people (like pimps and procurers) who derive illegitimate and unearned incomes from the women's labor.

It is important to take these elements in the Liberal agenda into consideration to understand why Feminists who subscribe to it have found common cause with international organizations of sex workers, probably more than any of the other groups of Feminists. Their thesis of freedom of work and legal protection accords well with the dominant viewpoint in "the International Whores Movement", an organized body that claims to represent sex workers the world over. Even more important than the relationship with organized sex workers, as such, is that this strand of Feminism accords recognition to the importance of the views of the sex workers as a whole, even if this recognition is only rarely translated into a research strategy that includes listening to them (O' Neill, 1996). In a way, this recognition of the voice of the women is itself a necessary part of the Liberal Feminist strategy. That is because listening to the women is believed to help their mobilization, and without their mobilization the goals that Liberal Feminism has set for them would be difficult to achieve.

Equally noteworthy for the purposes of this study is the fact that Liberal Feminism clears commercial sex workers of accusation as corrupt and polluted humanity; but it does so only in so far as it refers to them as entrepreneurs instead of "bad girls". In other words, it rejects the name calling that has been directed at the women only by calling them by some other name, not by showing how they are not, indeed, corrupt or polluted. This is one of the things to which I want to call attention in this study. I will pick up the argument later.

The last, but by no means the least important, of the strands of Feminism that addresses itself to the question of commercial sex is the one that explains "prostitution" as a situation forced on women by their poverty. Like the other strands of Feminist thought, this one also locates the causes of the poverty that drives the women into "prostitution" in the male bias that prevails in society. In the case of this particular viewpoint, society's male-bias shows in its refusal or reluctance to recognize domestic service as work and in its refusal to remunerate the labor or service that women provide in that sphere. Its criticism is that there are double standards both in recognizing something as work and in paying for it. Because a whole range of work that women do at home is not recognized as work, it goes totally unpaid; it is unrecognized and unpaid even though all of it is "reproductive" work that directly subsidizes capital by preparing the male labor force for "productive" work (Malos, 1980; Jaget, 1980). The consequence of not recognizing and paying for "reproductive" work has been that poverty increasingly has come to take the form of female poverty. Women, in short, are disproportionately represented among the poor. For lack of alternative, many turn to commercial sex.

As regards its characterization of the women, this strand of Feminism is probably the most neutral, associating commercial sex-workers neither with gullibility in the face of patriarchal ideology nor with positive traits like entrepreneurship. For this group, the women are basically reacting to economic misery, nothing more nothing less.

In the world of action, this strand of Feminist thought is linked with movements like The International Wages for Housework Campaign, a campaign that advocates equal wages for housework and industrial work. These movements are predominantly organized and run by women who are not sex workers. However, it also involved in campaigns against laws enacted against commercial sex work under the slogan "Outlaw poverty and not prostitution". It makes common cause with the women in commercial sex and advocates the significance of listening to and bringing the women affected into the struggle. In short, it can be said that it is very similar to the Liberal Feminism in terms of strategy.

1.3 Beyond Patriarchy and Feminism: A Brief Critique of Western Literature

From the foregoing, several points emerge very clearly. One point is that, in the West, both sex work and the sex worker have been portrayed in many different ways. The other point is that the characterization of the "prostitute" depended on how decision-makers, activists or scholars understood the institution of "prostitution" and accounted for its existence in society, although it cannot be said that negative portrayals of sex workers always followed condemnations of "prostitution" as an institution or that positive portrayals of sex workers always implied approval of "prostitution". Broadly speaking, the major line of difference has been between the male-centered discourse on "prostitution" and associated characterizations of the "prostitutes" on the one hand, and the female-centered discourse on "prostitution" and associated characterizations of the "prostitute" on the other. Generally, it can be said that the male-centered reflections tended to be critical of "prostitutes" and less critical of "prostitution" whereas the female-centered reflections tended to be more critical of "prostitution" and less critical of "prostitutes".

However, I am much more interested in this study in what is strikingly common to both kinds of reflection. That common element is the fact that the "prostitutes", or the "sex workers" as the case may be, are always taken as if they constitute a single, undifferentiated, social entity. While they are studied for what separates them from other women or for what make them similar to other women, they are not studied as a social category in their own right. The verdicts that came down from the various perspectives are that either "prostitutes" were "bad people" or that "sex workers" are not bad people, but these verdicts came without a focused study of the variety of forms that commercial sex work takes and the various ways in which women with different backgrounds adjust to its different forms. In short, neither "prostitution" as a social institution, nor "prostitutes" as a social category, are unpacked and differentiated. In this regard, it is important not to confuse different ways of *conceptualizing* "prostitution" or "prostitutes" with *differentiating* both the institution and the practitioners *internally*. While the voluminous literature on both of them is a result of different perspectives and different judgments, the literature that seeks to understand them from within is amazingly thin. I would have said that such a literature does not exist at all, but this would not be entirely correct because there are works, mostly in the Liberal Feminist camp, that make some attempt at classifying "prostitutes" into "types" or "classes" on the basis of where they go to work and describing their mobility across these "types" and "classes".

It is reasonable, therefore, to conclude that decision-makers, activists or scholars be they male-biased or female-biased, operated with the notion that the very fact of engaging in commercial sex endowed "prostitutes" with a distinct identity, a distinct set of behaviors and attitudes; this identity, set of behaviors and attitudes might be negatively or positively described; they might be read as radically marking off the women from all other women or not; but that they existed is assumed and that it arose from the fact of selling sex is taken for granted.

2 African Images and Approaches: From the Cultural Rebel to the Sexual Entrepreneur

One of the conspicuous absences in the literature on the African sex worker is the theme of "prostitution as pathology". The socio-biological argument that women turn to "prostitution" due to some kind of biological or psychological problem is not seriously taken in the Africanist literature. This is true even though the "relationship" between crime and "prostitution" is widely recognized. As stated by a student of commercial sex work in the Ugandan capital, Kampala (Bakwesegha, 1982: xvii), the overall tendency in the African literature seems to be actually to explain in cultural terms what Western literature explains in physical or biological terms.

> The [biological or] psychological incapacities purported by Western scholars to be the primary cause of prostitution ought to be seen and appreciated more as symptoms, rather than as causes, which the woman who indulges in prostitution suffers when she, on reflection, realizes the seriousness of the fact that [what she does]...is not the best expected of her by the larger "moral" society...

As the quote above suggests, primarily the "prostitute" in Africa is regarded as a cultural rebel. There is much more, however, to the theme of culture in the literature from Africa regarding the sex worker. Where the woman is not described as an alienated person, she is often described as a woman not constrained by cultural codes that govern the behaviors of others. In fact, this "freedom" of the "prostitute" in Africanist literature is often linked to the history of migration, so that the "prostitute" is not only a woman who has broken society's code of sexual conduct but is also a person who has broken away from the clutches of patriarchal culture by physically moving out of the countryside and coming to the city (Cohen, 1969; Emecheta, 1979).

Another sub-theme on the general theme of culture and the sex worker in Africa was the portrayal of the "prostitute" as a member of a counter-culture characterized by decadence and desolation. The only slight difference from the Western view in this regard is that African views emphasize the Western origins of this counter-culture, the belief being that "prostitution" itself was introduced by Europeans during colonial rule. This was a perspective quite common in the late colonial period or in the early years of African independence when cultural nationalism was at its height. In fact, revolutionary efforts in some newly liberated African countries that sought to rid society of cultural corruption by the West included campaigns to eradicate "prostitution" (Mullings, 1976).

Economic explanations of "prostitution" in Africa have likewise been very common. Most of the literature in this context is either part of the critique of colonial economic systems and their legacies for post-liberation Africa or is a product of Feminist perspectives on gender and socioeconomic structures. The literature draws both on Marxist perspectives and on Liberal Feminist perspective, the way a particular writer goes depending on his/her theoretical/ideological leanings.

Those with Marxist leanings focus on the impoverishment of women that attended the expansion of capitalism in the continent. Colonial economic systems favored African males for training and jobs in general, and for steady and better-paying jobs in particular. Women were integrated into the colonial economy as marginal elements, working in the informal sector as providers of service and comfort for the male labor force. Commercial sex, often associated with trade in alcoholic beverages, was the occupation into which women were pushed as a result (Van Onselen, 1982). The post-independence period, it is argued, did not change this imbalance in any significant way. In what appears to be reminiscent of Marx's metaphorical use of "prostitution" as a subjugation of one section of society by the other, there is a radical Africanist perspective in which the position which the "prostitute" occupies is sometimes likened to the marginal position which entire societies, not just women, occupy in an international system dominated by the West. In fact, in African creative literature "the prostitute" has frequently served as a metaphor for the most downtrodden sections of society who, on that account, are in the forefront of the struggle against oppression or foreign domination (LaPin, 1984).

Writers with Liberal Feminist leanings focus on "prostitution" as an economic enterprise, complete with calculations of cost, profit and investment strategies (Bujra, 1975, White, 1990). Luise White's study of the links between "prostitution" and the housing business in colonial Nairobi is a case in point (White, 1990). In Africa, as in the West, Feminist analyses of "prostitution" as an economic enterprise are critical of the criminalization of the business in the name of the well being of the public. Recent studies within this perspective are pointing out the significance of rescuing the personalities and the social worth of women who, only because they make a living in "prostitution", have been cast as embodiments of pollution and deviance (White, 1990).

Overall, the literature on "prostitution" in Africa is highly varied, just like the literature on "prostitution" in the West. Each author's portrayal of the "prostitute" is likewise related to what he/she takes as the principal cause of "prostitution". However, in the light of my objectives in this study, what is important to note is that, as in Western literature, the "Prostitute" in Africanist literature is also presented in collective and categorical terms. When it is not the cultural rebel, it is the decadent and loose woman; when it is not the poor migrant woman, it is the intrepid entrepreneur. What is missing is the differentiation of the category called "prostitute". What is also missing is an effort to establish what specific conditions arise in the social world surrounding life in "prostitution" in Africa. If in the West the "prostitute" is conceived as a highly individualistic person, engaged in competitive and largely adversarial relationships with varying groups of people, it may be in part due to the individualistic social order in that part of the world. In Africa, however, it is clear that ties of kinship and community have always been very strong, and that these ties tend to continue to be strong despite apparently disruptive phenomena like urbanization, migration or poverty. It is therefore a major weakness of the literature in Africa to relate the study of commercial sex work with these specificities. Arguments that de-link the "prostitute" from society at the moment she boards a bus to go to town, as if she never turns her face back to the countryside or arguments that describe "prostitutes" as lone figures wasting away in liquor and disease as if they cease to be women and therefore cease to produce children for whom they might have to care, do not take us very far. In short, what is missing in the literature in Africa is what Joanna Phoenix has recently called "the ethnography of prostitution" (Phoenix, 1999:3). For Africa, this "ethnography" has to be done both at a different level and with a higher degree of sensitivity than for the West.

3   Ethiopian Images and Approaches: Rural Women Lost in Town

Commercial Sex has been an important and attractive topic for sociological research in Ethiopia. Interest in the topic, which goes back to the 1960s (Mayor, 1962, 1963; Andargatchew, 1967; Lema, 1968), has increased in leaps and bounds since the end of the 1970s and the beginning of the 1980s (Laketch, 1978, 1991; Banchiyeleku, 1984; Ayehunie, 1987; Mehret, 1990; Habtamu, 1991; Baardson, 1993; Kebede, 1993; Tamene, 1993; Atakilt, 1994; Gedu, 1995; Alemayehu, 1996; Aklilu, 1998; Hussein, 1998; Seble, 1998; Mulumebet, 2000, Bethlehem, 2000, 2002). However, with a few outstanding exceptions (notably that of Laketch, 1978, 1991, Andargatchew, 1988 and Bethlehem, 2000, 2002) this research has displayed three common characteristics that are defined by the themes and approaches that were preferred and the common conclusions that were reached.

In terms of themes, research on commercial sex in Ethiopia had tended to be highly repetitive. It appears that this was partly a result of lack of integration, by which I mean that research projects were often not related to each other or did not refer to each other much. In fact, most of the literature consisted of unpublished reports prepared for government agencies or small-scale studies by students to fulfill degree requirements (Baardson, 1993; Mulumebet, 2000; Alemayehu B, 1996; Alemayehu M, 1973; Banchiyeleku, 1984; Habtamu, 1991; Tamene, 1993; Aklilu, 1998; Atakilt, 1994; Ayehunie, 1987; Gedu, 1995; Hussein, 1998; Kebede M, 1993; Kebede Y, 1980; Lemma, 1968; Seble, 1998; Tesfahunegn, 1990).

This "decentralized" research had tended to test the same themes over and over again with an ever-increasing number of samples. The favorite themes or issues have been "causes of prostitution", "types of prostitution" and "consequences of prostitution" (Alemayehu B, 1996; Alemayehu M, 1973; Banchiyeleku, 1984; Habtamu, 1991; Seble, 1998, Tamene, 1993). However, there has been very little attempt to integrate these themes and show them in their interrelationship. Only in very few of the studies do we have attempts to show the ways in which "the causes" of "prostitution" relate to the "types" (Laketch, 1978, 1991) but almost none exist where the implications of this data are worked out for the "consequences of prostitution" for both society and the women themselves.

Except in the context of "the causes", very little effort has been made to place commercial sex in the context of wider socio-economic conditions or processes or to explore other themes that have direct or indirect bearing on commercial sex (For exceptions see Laketch, 1978 and Andargatchew, 1988). Society, in other words, comes up for criticism often in connection with the factors that drive women to "prostitution", like early marriage and the lack of opportunity for women in the countryside. "Society" is not interrogated in connection with what happens to the women who are already in the sex business. What has severely limited the explanatory power as well as the practical value of studies of "prostitution" in Ethiopia is the underlying assumption that "prostitution" is something that only the "prostitute" does. Brief mentions here and there notwithstanding, the literature fails miserably to show the part played in it by the procurers and the employers of the women, or by the men who purchase sexual services. Nor does it consider the role of the state and its various agencies, certainly not in terms of what they might be doing in terms of facilitating and expanding the practice. The ritual listing of "consequences and recommendations" does not have much to contribute due to these failures to understand the problem of commercial sex comprehensively.

The literature is also highly repetitive in terms of approach or methodology. With very few exceptions, the most common approach has consisted of case studies of often very small samples of prostitutes through questionnaire-based structured surveys (Banchiyeleku, 1984; Habtamu, 1991; Gedu, 1995). Consequently, researchers have not only focused on quantitative evidence at the expense of qualitative evidence but also have tended to take commercial sex workers as objects rather than subjects of study.

The analysis of the quantitative data also left much to be desired. In many cases, one observes that a great deal of the evidence that came through even in the surveys was discarded because differences of a few percentage points would make certain pieces of evidence "not statistically significant". In other words the quantitative emphasis of the methodology has imposed a sort of statistical tyranny on the analysis.

Because of these kinds of methodological biases, the "findings and conclusions" about "prostitution" often sound like they had been pre-conceived and predictable. They portray "prostitution" as an "evil" practice that has negative moral, social, economic, and health consequences for society as a whole. They all raise various levels of alert against it with recommendations varying from the virulently abolitionist to the moderately regulationist.

Be that as it may, the main drawback of "prostitution" studies in Ethiopia is that most of them fail to clearly or consistently distinguish the institution, *as an institution*, from the women who find themselves in it one way or the other. Only the very few that are sympathetic to the women do so, and almost always these ones portray them as victims of an evil institution. As victims, sex workers were presented as illiterate women who had been either forced out of their birth places by bad socio-cultural practices or innocently dragged into the major cities by selfish or careless relatives. They were also presented as helpless people who had been denied alternative means of employment or livelihood. For most writers, however, the women themselves figure as embodiments of the evil itself. As such, they were castigated as promoters of alcoholism and other anti-social activities and primarily as major conduits of diseases that ravage society.

In fact, another overall characteristic of the literature on commercial sex in Ethiopia has been the fact that commercial sex is framed primarily as a public health problem. It is hardly possible to find a study of "prostitution" that does not make a reference to this dimension. More than any other idea, the idea that has most frequently figured in studies of commercial sex was that of impurity or pollution. This was, without doubt, a reflection of the fact that public or government bodies were likewise concerned primarily by the danger that commercial sex apparently posed to the health of the public. It was with this background of themes, approaches and conclusions that Ethiopian scholarship on commercial sex has picked up the issue of HIV and AIDS (Kebede, 1993; Atakilt, 1994; Hussein, 1998).

However, it is not the fact that "prostitution" tends to be taken as a close cousin of epidemiology that is of major concern for me in this study. It is the fact that the women who practice commercial sex are themselves held responsible for spreading the disease, that they are held responsible more than other sections of society, and that they are held responsible collectively. Because there is very little attempt to differentiate commercial sex and commercial sex workers to start with, there is very little attempt to differentiate among the women in relation to the type of commercial sex work that they do. Because this is not done, the interface between commercial sex and sexually transmitted diseases continues to elude researchers and activists.

The other striking characteristic of the material on commercial sex in Ethiopia is the fact that the typical image of the "prostitute" continues to be that of the migrant female. This continues to be the case despite the fact that over the last hundred years several generations of Ethiopians have lived in the cities and towns (Assefa, 1993). Existing literature has very little to say about non-migrant, intra-urban "prostitution", except a mention here and there that it does exist. It has, as a result, failed to show the connections between the institution and urban manifestations of phenomena like poverty, education, the family, and community life. For instance, existing studies of urban poverty in Addis Ababa or elsewhere (Girma, 1997; Yassin, 1997) do not explore its connections with "prostitution".

This review of the Ethiopian literature on commercial sex will not be complete if the exceptional contribution of Laketch Dirasse (1978, 1991) and Andargatchew Tesfaye (1988) is not recognized. Laketch's work stands out for its pioneering attempt to look a little more closely both at the institution of commercial sex and at the women who live in it. Most of Andargatchew's observations pertain to the institution rather than to the women who practice it. When it comes to the women Andargachew makes a very valuable contribution by expanding and improving upon the work of classification ventured into earlier by Laketch. He does so both by adding and subtracting types on the original findings of Laketch and by expanding the data for the whole of the country.

I believe that any effort to enrich our understanding of the lives and the concerns of the women behind commercial sex in Ethiopia has to build on the invaluable contributions of these two scholars. One way of doing so is to shift the focus of research even more towards the women themselves and to bring to the foreground their *emic* descriptions of life behind commercial sex. The other is to highlight the social dimensions of

42

this life by taking it beyond the work place. Both of these approaches involve the work of updating the typology of commercial sex workers, something on which both Laketch and Andargatchew have each done a good job.

I have set myself this task in this study. Accordingly, I will reopen the issue of classification of sex workers in the following chapter and set the stage for a differentiated analysis of the social world of sex workers in Addis in the fourth chapter.

Chapter Three

Towards Explaining Variety:
Perspectives on the Classification of Sex Work and Sex Workers in Addis Ababa

There is what appears to be an endless variety of sex work in Addis Ababa. Likewise, there is what appears to be an endless variety of sex workers. Previous researchers have reiterated this point (Laketch, 1978; Andargatchew, 1988). The general implication from previous listings of "types" of "prostitutes" is that there is hardly any category of womanhood in Addis Ababa that is not tainted somehow by the practice; there is no work place, school, or place of entertainment that did not include women who operated as undercover "prostitutes". By implication, again, there is hardly any form of conjugal or domestic arrangement between men and women, be it courtship, marriage or the family, that is not subverted by "prostitution" because of part-time engagement in it by the girlfriends, the wives or the daughters of otherwise decent men. To give a sense of how pervasive a practice "prostitution" was believed to have become and how much potentially subversive of the social fabric it was believed to be, it is worth quoting the statements by one close observer of the scene:

> ...these days it is becoming difficult to distinguish who is [a prostitute and] who [is not a prostitute]...Can anything be done to control the problem before it starts knocking at every door and further destabilize the family system? Can we any more afford to stand and watch? Are our young daughters and sisters safe? Can we dare answer these questions positively and live with clear conscience? (Andargatchew, 1988: 311-312).

One would have thought, as I did when I began this study, that by limiting the definition of sex worker to only those women who practice it openly and full-time, it is possible to work around this all-inclusive conception of "prostitution" and to come up with a concise and manageable list of "types" of commercial sex workers in the city. This does indeed reduce the complications somewhat, although, as I will show

44

below, it does not make the task as simple and straightforward as one might expect.

In this chapter I will propose a different approach to the classification of sex workers in Addis Ababa, an approach that I believe to be particularly helpful to capture the social context in which the women live their lives behind commercial sex. This approach will be different from previous approaches because it goes beyond the venue of work or the conditions of work, the two criteria that were focused on by previous scholars.

However, to set the stage for my attempt to differentiate sex workers as well as to highlight some of the components of previous typologies that I find to be useful for my own attempt, I will start by describing and discussing these previous typologies on the basis of the works of Laketch Dirasse (1978) and Andargatchew Tesfaye (1988). After that, I will introduce a scheme on which my own differentiation is based. My scheme will be based on five distinct variables, each of which contains several criteria under it. When taken individually, each of these variables explains one or another aspect of social life among a specific category of sex workers. When brought together, the variables account for the social context of virtually all the current forms of commercial sex work in Addis Ababa.

1 Laketch Dirasse's Classification of Sex Workers in Addis Ababa

Based on a sample of respondents that included 200 commercial sex workers, Laketch Dirasse has worked out a classification of Addis Ababa's sex workers as things stood at the time of her fieldwork in 1973-74. She states that her classification was "mostly derived" from the *emic* categories used by the women themselves as well as by "Ethiopians in Addis Ababa" in referring to sex workers. These categories, according to her, primarily took into account the places out of which the women operated, or, in her words, "the context within which they conduct their trade".

There were two "major categories" and six "categories" of sex workers in Addis Ababa, according to Laketch. The two major categories consisted of women for whom "prostitution" was the only source of income and women who supplemented their earnings from "prostitution" by selling liquor (p. 61). [1] Laketch lists the six categories of sex workers "in [an] ascending order of prestige and income".

The first category was that of "The Street Walkers". Women in this category tended to be "generally" very young and recent runaways from home; they were the "poorest" category of Addis Ababa's "prostitutes". For their services women in this group charged clients as low as 25 cents to a maximum of 2 Ethiopian *birr*.

The second category of women was what Laketch called "Kiosk Consorts". The distinctive mark of this group of women was that they lived and operated from small shacks or huts, marked off from other similar structures by red lights. In terms of income, this category of women was a bit better off than "The Street Walkers", netting an average of 44 Ethiopian *birr* per month.

After the "Kiosk Consorts" came the "Bar Consorts". She divides this group into two sub-categories, those working in the smaller clubs and bars and those working in the big bars. Women in the former sub-category usually received free room and board but no salary payments while those in the latter subcategory received a salary "which varies according to the girl's attractiveness". Laketch says that the women in this category earn an average monthly income of about 65 birr after "the bed charge" deductions.

Next to the "Bar Consorts" were a category made up of what Laketch called "Freelance Consorts". This category of women worked in the nightclubs frequented by the city's elite and by foreigners. Their term of engagement at the nightclubs was that they dance and encourage customers to consume drinks, nothing more. In return for this, they enjoyed benefits that included transportation services to and from their homes. The earnings of this group of women varied a great deal, according to Laketch, depending on whether the customers were local people or foreign tourists and diplomats. Overall, their average monthly income amounted to about 200 *birr*.

After the "Freelance Consorts" came two categories of women whom Laketch calls "Madames". What these two categories of women shared in common was the fact that they were successful entrepreneurs who also doubled as liquor traders. Laketch justifies dividing them into

---

[1] "And from the sex work of others" Laketch should have added, because in her subsequent analysis she says that one subcategory of liquor traders also collects a proportion of the income of the women they employ as "bed fee".

two categories as "Pettty-Madames" and "Madames" on the grounds that first, the former were less wealthy than the latter and, second, the former consisted of lone operators while the latter were employers of other women. The lone-operator "Petty-Madams" netted an average income of around 168 birr from both "prostitution" and liquor trade. The "Madames", who stood at the top of the hierarchy, engrossed an average income of upwards of 2,000 birr from their "triple sources of income", namely "their liquor trade, the percentage they get from the young bar-consorts who work under them, and what they make from their own clientele" (p.61).

It is difficult to ascertain, retrospectively, if Laketch's list of categories accounted for all the different forms of sex work in the city in the early 1970s. As we shall see below, Andargatchew believes that it did not, although he was writing about a decade later after the Revolution of 1974 had changed a number of things. In any case, much more important than the length of any list is the comprehensiveness of the criteria that was used for the classification and the ways in which the categories that resulted from the classification sustain themselves in as many of the "stories" as one wants to tell about commercial sex in Addis Ababa. Laketch primarily wanted to tell an economic (occupational) story of commercial sex in Addis Ababa. Given her emphasis on this dimension, it is quite understandable that her primary criteria of classification consisted of the place of work and the conditions of work of the women. In other words, it is understandable that Laketch's work meets the women primarily at the point where they make money from selling sex. Laketch's ranking of the women is also based purely on their performance at the moneymaking line. Although she uses the phrase "income and prestige" to describe her criteria for the ranking, it becomes quickly apparent, from the details that she provides, that she is in fact referring to "prestige based on income". Despite her statement elsewhere that certain Ethiopian cultures tolerate or condone "prostitution", she is not implying that women become socially "prestigious" as "prostitutes".

In short, the classification of commercial sex workers is deployed by Laketch to tackle only a small range of issues in and around the "kiosks", the bars, and the nightclubs where she found and talked to the women. Thus, even if we take it as a complete list of categories in terms of the economics of the work, it can hardly be taken as a complete list in terms of its social context. Her attempt to differentiate the women, in short, is

47

not comprehensive enough to take full account of "prostitution" as a socioeconomic phenomenon.

2 Andargatchew Tesfaye's Classification of Sex Workers in Addis Ababa

A mild critique of Laketch's classification exists in Andargatchew Tesfaye's work. I say mild critique because Andargatchew refrains from going into the evaluation of Laketch's classification. Instead, he prefers to point out the few places where he believes she might have been incorrect and proceeds to rework the list. As he does so, he adds and subtracts from her list, while renaming and/or redefining those that he keeps. Thus he drops the two categories of "Madams" from Laketch's list because "it does [not] appear there is any need to classify the "madams" as a separate group" (p. 302). Furthermore, he also takes her "Free Lancers" off the list, stating that "the type of night-clubs she refers to do not seem to exist anymore". He substitutes Laketch's two categories of "Madames" and the "Free Lancers" with his own "two more types", which, in fact, are three. These new "types" are "closed door prostitutes", women who engage in "prostitution" as "a side-business", and "prostitutes who work "clandestinely" (pp.308-312).

First on Andargatchew's list are the Street Walkers. The second category is the "Kiosk Prostitutes". By and large, Andargatchew keeps many of the elements in Laketch's description of this category, with the exception of their earnings.

The next category in Andargatchew's list is made up of women who work out of small drinking places. These are, apparently, Laketch's "Petty-Madams" although the characteristics that Andargatchew associates with them vary somewhat from those suggested by her. Whereas for Laketch the women "own small drinking places like bars, coffee shops and groceries" (p.59), for Andargatchew, they were "women who sell local drinks like *arake*, beer, soft drinks". Equally interesting is that for Laketch the women in this category had a reasonably good income (p.59), while for Andargatchew they are lower class types who "supplement their income from the sale of cheap types of drinks", and "usually cater to the needs of people in the lower income groups" (p. 304).

Following these lone operators in Andargatchew's list were "Prostitutes in Bars and Coffee Shops". This is a category in which he includes some elements of Laketch's "Free Lancers" and "Madams" but describes a significantly different organization of both the place and the terms of work so that, in effect, it becomes an entirely different category. To begin with, the owners of these bars are owned by madams "who may or may not prostitute", and this depended on their age and marital status. Secondly, there were significant variations among the bars themselves, "depending on the size of the bar and on whether the bar combines dancing on a daily or occasional basis."(p. 304). These variations in the size and nature of the bars correlated with the two sub-categories of commercial sex workers, who collectively were referred to as xššôC ("ashashachoch", i.e. sales helpers).

In the first sub-category of "ashashachoch" were women who worked in bars that sold drinks but did not include dancing. These women were paid small salaries and obtained room and board. Their task was to have customers consume as much drinks as possible and to encourage the men to buy them drinks too. In some cases the women were motivated in this business with commission payments on the amount of drink that they helped sell while in some cases they pretended to be drinking alcohol but consumed "some kind of mixture", thereby boosting the sales through fraud. Andargatchew says that whether or not the women shared with the madams their incomes from selling sex depended on their contract with them; it was thus apparently not a universal practice (pp.304-305). It is noteworthy, however, that Andargachew's list shifts the focus in this context from the Madams who own the places to the women who work for them.

In the second sub-category of women who worked in the bars were women who were neither paid nor given board. These women usually worked in bars that also combined liquor trade with dancing. The women reported to work on a daily basis and engaged in the task of encouraging customers to drink "either through their charm or by out-dancing customers to exhaustion and thus increasing their desire for more drinks."(p. 306). This group of "ashashachoch" kept all their earning from selling sex and might, in some cases, even be rewarded with payment from the sales of drinks that they made possible. The women in this subcategory tended to be young "but 'sophisticated'" girls. There were procurers who recruited these women for the bars from among "run-away girls from the provinces or local school drop-outs."

49

In the fifth category in Andargatchew's typology were women who sold sex out of "small hotels cum drinking places". The women in this category worked and lived under conditions described above for bar girls, the only difference in this case being that the women are paid a salary of about 50 *birr* or more and always paid the hotel owner something every time they found clients. The payment was mandatory irrespective of whether the women used the beds in the hotel or not. Their living conditions were also generally very crowded, apparently deliberately "so that the girls make sure they get customers for the night ensuring that the hotel rooms are rented out" (p. 306).

The three categories of women whom Andargatchew adds to the list of sex workers can, in fact, be grouped together as women who practiced commercial sex under one or another kind of disguise. His categories are based either on the mode of operation of the women or on the social groups out of which the women usually came. In the first category were "closed door" "prostitutes" who catered to a select, rich and powerful clientele, including expatriates. The women operated out of villas or apartments to which customers were conducted by "pimps" or through word of mouth. The women engaged in liquor trade without license, supplied most probably through the black market or duty free channels and charged, consequently, exorbitant prices. Some of the women had other regular jobs and practiced part-time, but most were full-timers.

The second category consisted of women who engaged in "prostitution" as a side business "to supplement their incomes". Andargatchew notes that there were two subcategories of these. The first were office workers or otherwise employed women who "may not necessarily [be] poorly paid" (p. 309). In fact some of them might be well off already, owning cars and other property. Their engagement in commercial sex is aimed at making significant amounts of money. Their mode of operation ranged from going to big hotels in the hope of landing foreigners or parking their cars in front of drinking places waiting for pickup by men. Some operated from their homes through "pimps", go-betweens or even taxi drivers.

The second subcategory of women who engaged in "prostitution" on the side consisted of blue-collar types, lowly paid workers in produce- or service-oriented industries. Usually, these women tended to be of rural origin. Having come to the cities in search of employment, nonetheless found that income from their jobs was not enough; they therefore doubled in the business selling drinks or sex or both. Andargatchew notes that in several places, notably in the industrial suburbs of Addis Ababa such as Akaki and Kaliti, these women were associated with security problems caused by late-night altercations between them and their clients (pp. 309-310).

Finally come what Andargatchew calls a highly invisible "eighth type of prostitution". "Many people concerned with the problem of prostitution are very reluctant to admit" the existence of this type, he says (p.310). The "prostitutes" who practice this type were school or college girls, who, according to a local magazine he quotes, are "tempted" into the trade by "foreigners as well as Ethiopians". Andargatchew says that, due to its clandestine nature, the volume of this type of "prostitution" is difficult to measure. Accordingly, he does not have much to say about its specific characteristics (Ibid).

From the foregoing, I think it is useful to take note of an important improvement that Andargatchew's typology represents on that of Laketch, an improvement to which I like to draw attention because I seek to pursue it in my own efforts to classify sex workers below. Andargatchew's typology, unlike that of Laketch, includes elements outside of the place where commercial sex occurs. He includes elements like the origins of the women (urban or rural), their motives for becoming "prostitutes" and, at least in one case, living conditions outside the place of work. All of these elements, I believe, are very important variables for a comprehensive differentiation of the sex worker population and should be expanded on.

An important point of difference between the typologies of Andargatchew and Laketch is the fact that the categories listed by the former, unlike those listed by the latter, do not reflect a hierarchy among the women who practice commercial sex. The fact that some women who engage in "prostitution" had other lines of employment, or that they have money or property, did not suggest to Andargatchew that they were, merely on that account, better than other "prostitutes". There is no mention of the word "prestige" in Andargatchew's work, let alone hierarchies of "prestige" among sex workers.

I think it is also important to note that Andargatchew's typologies reflect conditions existing at the time of his writing. The onset of the Ethiopian Revolution in 1974 was followed by efforts to enforce a new public morality characterized, among other things, by the persecution and discouragement of certain kinds of public entertainment and leisure. Nightclubs were, for instance, banned. There was even a time when drinking during the day and renting hotel rooms with women who are not one's wives was prohibited. I think that it was these kinds of measures that account, in part, for the absence of some of the major types of commercial sex activity, such as freelancing with nightclubs, in Laketch's classification.

However, it is also clear that the Revolution did not achieve its goals of establishing a new regime of public morality. What it actually achieved was pushing some of the pre-revolution forms of entertainment and leisure underground. This, I think, is what accounts for the emergence of the types of commercial sex work that figure in Andargatchew's work but not in that of Laketch.

3 Towards A Comprehensive Differentiation: Work, Residence and other Socioeconomic Variables

In the remainder of this chapter, I will present a scheme of differentiation based primarily on the variables that determine the social behavior of the women who practice commercial sex in Addis Ababa today. This scheme, I believe, is helpful not only to identify the major categories of commercial sex workers but also to account for further differentiation within each category. It is a scheme that seeks to answer two major questions: why do women who practice particular types of commercial sex work engage in social ties, in social institutions or in social processes that women who practice other types of commercial sex work do not engage in? What factors, other than the type of commercial sex work that they practice, determine the social personalities of sex workers both in relation to each other and in relation to others?

It can be said that the first question relates to social behavior shared by all women in one category while the second question relates to differences in social behavior within each category, differences that can be described either as social behaviors of sub-categories or as social behaviors of individuals. Of course, there are a number of reasons why social behaviors of women in one category tend to harmonize and for which, therefore, further differentiation of social behavior in terms of sub-categories and individuals should not be taken too far. Women with similar social background *tend* to take up similar kinds of sex work, which then *tends* to shape the way they socialize among themselves as well as with others. However, there are many significant exceptions to these general *tendencies* and they have to be accounted for. For, it is also possible for women with very different social backgrounds to find themselves engaging in the same type of commercial sex work and, due to those different backgrounds, to socialize differently both among themselves and with other people. Nor should it be forgotten that different kinds of social ties develop between commercial sex workers and other people *after* the latter had taken up a particular type of sex work. These ties also affect the way the women socialize both with the women in a similar line of work and with other people. In short, the social behavior of women who do sex work is determined not just by the type of sex work they do but also by their background and by what happens between them and other people outside of the workplace.

Given this, it can be said that there are both potential advantages and disadvantages in taking the type of sex work as a chief variable to categorize sex workers. The potential advantages are that it is relatively simple and that it accounts for many of the similarities in the women's social behavior. The latter point is particularly important because working out similarities enables us to bring some order into the apparent chaos that will necessarily follow if we were to take every sex worker as an individual social animal. The potential disadvantages are that it might simplify the problem too much and that it might result in a work of pigeonholing that does not take full account of complex reality.

The scheme that I propose below seeks to keep the potential advantages of work-based differentiation while guarding against its potential disadvantages. I will try to do so by doing two things: one is being as comprehensive as possible about the types of sex work that are practiced and the sub-types within each type of sex work; the other is by bringing in other variables that have various degrees of significance in determining the social engagement of the women *independently of the type of sex work that they do*. I have identified four of these variables. They are: personal and family background, expressed reasons for becoming a sex worker, place and condition of residence, and involvement in social ties based on relationship of dependence.

Anybody familiar with the literature on commercial sex in Ethiopia will note that I am not the first person to have compiled data on the fist two of these variables, namely, background of the women and expressed reasons for becoming a sex worker. Previous researchers have collected a great deal of statistical information on both. However, this will be the first time that such data have been integrated with information on the types of sex work to come up with a comprehensive differentiation of the sex worker population in Addis Ababa. However, the last two variables, namely, place and condition of residence and involvement in relationships of dependence, have not attracted much attention from previous researchers. Due to the focus on what sex workers do at work rather than on what they do after work, they have not been found to be important bodies of information about both the institution and the women connected with it. Even where something related to these variables was mentioned, it was always done anecdotally and briefly, not structurally or in detail. I will give details below on all the four variables and the dynamics that each one of them brings into our attempt to understand comprehensively the social world of sex workers.

However, before I proceed, I think it is useful to explain how I arrived at this scheme and why I think it is valid. The scheme is based on information that I collected from women who openly acknowledge that they are commercial sex workers. In fact, I could say that it was the women themselves who suggested the scheme to me, except that they did so only indirectly by responding to my probing questions rather than directly. What I would like to claim for this scheme, as Laketch did for her typology nearly thirty years ago, is that it is very much *emic*. The difference in this case may be that it is deliberately and very self-consciously so. It involved a great deal of struggle with the *ethic*, because the *ethic*, at least as we know it so far, discouraged any kind of further probing into "prostitution" or "prostitutes" because both the institution and the women were taken as units of analysis rather than as elements to be analyzed.

The validity of my scheme also rests, I believe, primarily on its intelligibility to the women who are living the lives that I am trying to explicate. It is a representation that any of the women that I worked with would understand and easily relate to if it were to be presented to her in Amharic, the language in which she and her friends had communicated it to me.

What a given woman who practices commercial sex in Addis Ababa can or cannot do (or actually does or does not do) in the social sphere depends on five distinct variables, each of which makes an important contribution to the solution of the puzzle about her social behavior even though none of them can solve the puzzle alone. I will call these variables "Background" "Entry" "Work", "Residence" and "Dependence". For a great majority of sex workers that I have talked to, the order in which these variables are put here parallels the course that their lives have taken. Typically a sex worker would have grown up in a particular place and under specific conditions that would contribute to the direction that her future life takes (thus: background); then there would be one or a combination of precipitating factors that would push her into this kind of work (thus: entry); once on the job, she would be engaged in a particular type of commercial sex work (thus: work); although the circumstances of her work may or may not be directly tied to the circumstances of her residence, the place and the condition to which she retires after work would at least partly determine the social circuit within which she would move (thus; residence); finally, the woman may have maintained old relationships or may have developed new relationships with a specific category of people within which she either gives or takes resources as a matter of obligation (thus: dependence).

However, my discussion of the five variables below will not necessarily follow this order. In stead, I will begin with two variables that are the most significant in determining the circuit within which the women act socially. These variables are the place and condition of work and the place and condition of residence. The order in which I discuss the other variables does not imply any hierarchy at all. Yet, it is important to note that prioritizing the two variables of work and residence does not imply that all the others are dependent on these two. On the contrary, my chief argument in this chapter is that the other variables also have varying degrees of independence of their own for a classification scheme that focuses on the social behavior of the women.

Below, I will discuss each variable individually, presenting my findings on its frequency for my sample of 100 women. In the following chapter, I will present interface data and discuss the interrelationship between the variables by taking each type of sex work as a context for the discussion.

3.1 Types of Sex work in Addis Ababa: Venues and Conditions

If one were to pose to a sex worker in Addis Ababa a question like "What kind of sex worker are you?" the answer would very likely be something that refers to the type of sex work that she does. In other words, the first level of self-identification within the sex worker community relates the woman to one or another form of the sex business in town. Other levels of self-identification might refer to the woman's age, her education, her personal character or even ethnicity. But none of these levels come before the type of work that the woman does. Therefore, in any effort to classify the women into categories the first order of business should be identifying the various types of sex work that are practiced.

Types of sex work are also categories around which group consciousness is created among the women. By group, I am referring to informal, not formal groups. When a woman identifies herself with a particular type of sex work, she is also identifying herself with other women who are in a similar line of work. That identification could, of course, mean a number of things: it could mean acknowledging and sharing what are believed to be attributes of the group, attributes that could be negative or positive; it could mean acknowledging these attributes but refusing to share them with others; it could also mean refusing to acknowledge these attributes at all. My focus group discussions, which were organized on the basis of types of sex work the women practiced, have brought to the surface interesting differences of this kind among members of each category.

It should, however, be pointed out that, in some cases, women identify themselves with more than one type of commercial sex work. This element sometimes creates what can be called a problem of multiple identities. There are two possible solutions to this problem: one is to insist that the women identify a single type of work in which they engage frequently, and thus associate them with that type; the other is to categorize them separately as women who move between different types. In this study I have chosen the latter solution.

Sex workers in Addis Ababa refer to the types of sex work in which they engage on the basis of either of two things: venue or condition of work. Venue refers to the place where the woman meets her clients whereas condition of work refers to the terms under which the woman stays in the venue to wait for her clients. Venues vary considerably. They range from the women's own homes to business establishments like bars, drinking places, hotels or nightclubs. Venues could even be streets, although it is often unknown or overlooked that the streets are divided up among the women and "organized" as work places (more on this below).

Each venue of sex work is likewise associated with a particular combination of conditions under which the woman would operate from that place. In some venues, the conditions force the woman to use the place not only as a place of meeting her clients but also of delivering sexual services to them. Some others might force the women to share with owners of the establishment a certain percentage of their incomes from the service, irrespective of whether or not the service is delivered at the venue. Still others require the women to do other kinds of work for the owners of the venue as they wait for their clients. This work may or may not be remunerated, depending on the importance of the woman in bringing income to the place. There are venues where the women also live, in some cases with dependents. There are venues for which the women have to pay admission and others where they are required to spend money, like male customers, on drinks or food. As I will show below, there are a great variety of linkages between venues and terms of operation to which the women are subject. What is important to note at this point is that these linkages between venues and conditions are universal. Even though there may be a few venues where the terms or conditions of work are self-imposed or appear light and un-constraining, there is hardly any venue of sex work to which no conditions apply.

Despite this universal association between venues and conditions, the specific terms used by sex workers to refer to the type of sex work that they do could refer either to the venue or to the conditions only. From the responses to my questions about the type of sex work that women do, I have been able to identify seven distinct types, four referring to venues of work and the remaining three referring to conditions of work. The four types named after venues are አስፋልት (*asphalt*, i.e. work in the streets) መጠጥ:ቤት (*metet-bet*, i.e. work in small drinking places) ቡና:ቤት (buna-bet, i.e. work out of bars in small hotels) and ሆቴል/ክለብ (work out of big hotels and/or nightclubs). The three types named after conditions of work are bxLU (*be-alga*, literally work on one's bed, i.e. in one's home) እቁል:አካፋይ (*iqul-akafay*, i.e. work on the basis of 50% share with the owner of the house) and የተወሰነ:አካፋይ (*yetewosene-akafay*, i.e. work in which a fixed amount of money per session is handed over to the owner of the house).

Since, as I have stated above, venues are always associated with conditions and conditions are associated with venues, a full description of types of sex work in Addis Ababa necessarily requires matching these two elements for the seven types mentioned above. I will do this later in the chapter. But it is important to take note of the fact that one of the four types of sex work mentioned above in terms of venues, namely ሆቴል/ክለብ (hotel and/or night club) has a couple of distinctive things about it. First, it is actually a combination of two venues, namely big hotels and nightclubs. I put the two venues together partly because the women who go to one of the venues also go to the other and partly because the venues themselves sometimes combine both, as when nightclubs are located inside hotels. Secondly, this type sex work does not serve as a basis for self-identification by the sex workers themselves, at least not for the women in my sample.

There is no woman, for instance, who would say that she is a "hotel sex worker" or "a nightclub sex-worker" even if she spends a lot of time in these venues and meets her clients there. I think this is to be explained in terms of the manner in which sex work is conducted nowadays out of the big hotels and/or the nightclubs. The big hotels do not formally engage sex workers. They are not, therefore, mentioned along with those formal places of work to which the women go on a daily basis. Commercial sex operates in the big hotels informally, through linkages between staff, go-betweens, and the women. Likewise, nightclubs do not keep women on their payroll these days. The women arrive on their own as customers and have to order drinks in order to hang around in the premises. The informality of work in these two venues means that there is no regularity of attendance by the women, at least in the formal sense. It also means that women who work formally in other venues also go there sometimes. The most frequent "convertible" users of hotels and nightclubs are, for instance, the streetwalkers, who call themselves "asphalt-workers".

The types of sex work listed above can be put in some order based on the number of women in my sample who engage in each type. Accordingly, the most widely spread type, engaging the largest number of women is *yetewesene akafay*, i.e. work out of residences on the basis of fixed payments per session to the owner of the house). 35 out of my 100 respondents (35%) currently practice this variety. The second most important type, employing 25% of the women in the sample, is *asphalt*, or streetwalking. 12% of the women in the sample work *be-alga*, i.e. from rented houses of their own. 11% of the women were engaged in work that takes them to different places but principally to big hotels and nightclubs. 7% of the women reported that they work out of *buna-bet*, i.e. bars associated with small hotels. 5% were *iqul-akafay*, giving 50% of their earnings to the person who owns the place of work. Finally, 5% of my respondents use as venue the *metet-bet*, i.e. small drinking places.

It is difficult to make serious or valid inferences about the overall situation regarding sex work in Addis Ababa just from this list of types of work and the rough sketch of the proportion of sex workers that are engaged in each. Prior to making such inferences, it is important to have more detail on how each type of sex work is internally organized, what kinds of women each type attracts and what conditions or constraints each type imposes on the women involved in it. I will provide these details in the following chapter. In the remainder of this chapter, I will introduce the other variables that I believe are crucial to further elaborate and elucidate the material on venues and conditions of work.

3.2   Commercial Sex, Household and Domesticity

The interconnection between commercial sex work and housing is an issue that has not attracted as much attention as it deserves. The importance of housing arises not just from the simple fact that the women need shelter, just as much as they need food or clothing; it arises mainly from the fact that the different types of sex work in Addis Ababa are associated with different arrangements of residence, so that the decision that a woman makes to undertake one type of sex work is also a decision to enter into a specific form of residence. In fact, under conditions currently existing in the city, it is difficult to say whether it is the types of sex work that determine the residential arrangements or the residential arrangements that determine the types of sex work. I will pick up this problem later. But there is no doubt that, once a woman has entered one type of sex work, the conditions under which she works as well as her mobility within *and* between types of sex work are very much influenced, if not directly dictated, by the way work and housing are combined for her.

In some of the types of sex work, residence and work are brought together in one place; in other types they are separated. The major difference between the two is that where work and residence are combined, the organization of space for the two purposes is the responsibility of the employer (with the exception of the *be-alga* operators, while in those cases where work and residence are separated, the organization of residence, as a whole, is the task of the woman herself. However, both in those types where residence and work are combined and in those where they are separated, there are varying conditions of residence. In some of the types where the two are combined, for instance, the women have options as to where they want to reside; in some others, they don't have this option because work and residence may have to take place in the same house or even in the same room. There are, therefore, cases in which the combination of the two is structural and cases where it is not so structural.

In those types of sex work where residence is not directly linked to work, there are, likewise, many different arrangements of residence. There are some arrangements in which, despite separation, the work influences the form of residence indirectly. This happens when women who work together take up residence together, as roommates. The rental arrangements into which groups of sex workers enter also vary considerably, some permitting the women more freedom of use of the premises, others permitting them less freedom.

There could also be arrangements of residence in which the women make determined efforts to keep their work and their households separate. For some women the separation of work and household becomes a very crucial matter indeed, and the effort to ensure that this happens takes the form of maintaining two forms of identity: a work place identity and a residential identity.

Just as residence is related to work in many different ways, there are many different ways in which it is related to domesticity also. Women whose place of work and residence are separated could be living in domestic arrangements of various kinds. These might include marriage, but are often other forms of consensual partnership. Some of the young women who engage in commercial sex live with their parental families, and the members of their families may or may not know what they do outside of the house. There are women who are themselves parents or heads of families and that could be with or without male partners.

The most difficult arrangements, often full of agony and torment for the women, are those in which work, residence and domesticity are combined in one venue. There are women who try to accommodate sexual business and child rearing under a single roof, often in one tiny room; there are women who try to run a life of marriage and sex work under the same roof. Even if they are rare or uncommon, it is very important to study these extreme forms in which the women try to combine two elements that are almost impossible to combine. It is important because they show us two seemingly contradictory things at the same time: the ongoing tension between commercial sex and domestic life as well as the ways in which these two contradictory institutions accommodate each other.

The data on residence and its connections with work and domesticity were assembled partly from responses to relevant questions in the questionnaire, partly from the one-to-one interviews, from focus group discussions and from observation. The numerical data suggests that the majority of Addis Ababa's sex workers live where they work. 54% of the women in my sample said that their work place and their residence are connected whereas 46% said that they did not live where they worked. Very interestingly, only 5% of the women who lived where they worked said that living quarters and the venue at which they sold sex are separated. A striking 49% said that they lived and slept with clients in the same house or room. Of these respondents, the greatest majority (93%) said that they live and work in a house that individuals have rented from the government and have sublet to them or to their employers. Only 5 respondents (10.2%) said that the houses in which they lived and worked were directly rented from the government. 3 respondents (6.1%) said that they or their employers rented the houses from private owners.

Out of the 46 % of my respondents who said that they lived away from work, 19 (41.3%) lived by themselves, 10 (21.7%) lived with their parents, another 10 (21.7%) lived with friends as roommates, 4 (8.6%) lived with their siblings and 2 (4.3%) said that they lived with relatives. One respondent said that she does not have a fixed place of residence at all. While each of these figures is interesting for the points that I will later make for the social context of commercial sex, it should be noted that the women who said that they lived by themselves are not all saying that they lived alone. As we shall see below, this figure includes those respondents who live with one or more member of a nuclear family (consisting of spouse and children).

3.3   Socioeconomic Background and Demographic Data

Under this variable, I posited in my questionnaire five elements that I suspected to have relevance both for the decision of the respondent to take up commercial sex work and the social context in which she does the work: the age of the respondent, the marital history of the respondent, her place of origin, her upbringing (both in terms of the parental and the material sense of upbringing) and the level of formal education that the respondent had attained prior to entry into commercial sex.

Data on the age and the marital history of the respondent are important because it is believed that they relate to the reasons for which the women turn to commercial sex, to the type of sex work that each woman is likely to engage, and the social context in which she would operate once she has become a sex worker. It is also interesting to see what parallels exist between age and the different types of sex work in view of some conclusions along these lines made by previous scholars. Likewise, marital history has been frequently linked to the entry of women into commercial sex. It would be interesting to see how much of that holds true for Addis Ababa's sex workers currently.

My objective for posing questions on places of origin of the respondents was to see what proportion of Addis Ababa's commercial sex workers are indigenous to the city and what proportion are migrants. I hoped that this data might tell us something about the trends since the 1970s and the 1980s because the major studies conducted in the 70s and 80s have shown that most of the sex-worker population of Addis Ababa was made up of migrants to the city.

The thinking behind my inclusion of the element about upbringing is, likewise, that the conditions under which the respondent grew up might have some relationship to her decision to take up commercial sex as work and to the elements that sustain her in the work. Upbringing had two elements under it: the domestic (parental) conditions under which the respondent grew up and the material conditions of the household in which she grew up. The questions on parental conditions asked who raised the respondent whereas the questions on material conditions asked whether the household in which the respondent grew up could be described as rich, poor or self-sufficient.

I sought data on the level of formal education that the respondents had attained both to see what kind of correlation exists between lack of education and resort to commercial sex work and the degree to which the conclusions that previous studies have reached on this issue are still valid. Laketch, in particular, had found that the educational attainment of the sex workers in her sample was significantly high given Ethiopia's conditions at the time of her research. She had explained this in terms of the gender-bias in the job market.

My findings on these issues for all the women in my sample are as follows. Addis Ababa's sex workers are, overall, very young women. The average age reported for the 100 women in my sample is 23 years. There might, of course, be some under-reporting. But my own visual impression of the respondents is that more than 85% would be in their early 20s.

TABLE I

Cross Tabulation of Average Age and Categories of Commercial Sex Workers

Categories of Sex-workers	Percent (%)	Average Age (Years)
Fixed-share Sex-workers	35	21
Asphalt Sex-workers	25	22
Independent Home-based Sex-Workers	12	31
Sex-workers based in Hotels and Nightclubs	11	22
Sex-workers based in Bars	7	23
Equal-share Sex-workers	5	24
Sex-workers based in Drinking Places	5	29
Total	100	23

Even more striking, however, is the reported age of the women at the point of entering commercial sex. The data reveal that most of them (73%) started commercial sex as teenagers, and a significant number (11%) were actually children below the age of 15. 17% of my respondents were between the ages of 21-25 when they started and only 5% were over 25. Another 5% did not know what age they were when they started.

TABLE II

Cross Tabulation of Age at Entry and Categories of Commercial Sex
Workers (As Percent of Total within Each Category)

Categories of Sex-Workers	Age at Entry into Commercial Sex Work				
	<15	*16-20*	*21-25*	*>25*	*I don't know*
Fixed-share Sex-workers	17.1	65.7	8.6	2.8	5.7
Asphalt Sex-workers	16	60	16	8	0
Independent Home-based Sex-Workers	0	25	33.3	16.7	25
Sex-workers based in Hotels and Nightclubs	0	81.8	18.2	0	0
Sex-workers based in Bars	14.3	71.4	14.3	0	0
Equal-share Sex-workers	0	40	60	0	0
Sex-workers based in Drinking Places	0	100	0	0	0

The majority of Addis Ababa's sex workers today (65%) are women who were never married. Of the 35% who said that they were married, 33 individuals (94.2%) said that they were divorced prior to entry to commercial sex while 2 individuals (5.7%) said that they were widowed. Incidentally, only 3% of my respondents said that they were married more than once. All of those who were married prior to becoming sex workers were married below the age of 20. 10% were married below the age of 10; 17% were 10-15 years of age, whereas only 7% were aged 15-20.

One of my very interesting findings is that the majority of Addis Ababa's sex workers today are indigenous to the city. 52% of my respondents were both born and brought up in Addis Ababa as against 48% that came from outside. Of those who have migrated to the city only 24% were actually born and brought up in rural Ethiopia. What this means is that the vast majority, a total of 76%, originated from urban settlements of some kind, including small towns.

TABLE III

Place of Origin and Length of Stay in Addis Ababa of Commercial Sex-
Workers in Each Category (As Percent of Total within Each Category)

Categories of sex workers	Place of Origin		Length of stay in Addis Ababa					
	Addis Ababa	Outside Addis Ababa	Less than a year	1-3 years	3-5 years	5-7 years	7-10 years	Over 10 years
Fixed-share Sex-workers	31.4	68.6	0	17.1	14.3	2.9	22.9	11.4
Asphalt Sex-workers	72	28	0	4	4	0	4	16
Independent Home-based Sex-Workers	33.3	66.7	0	0	8.3	0	8.3	50
Sex-workers based in Hotels and Nightclubs	81.8	18.2	0	0	0	9.1	9.1	0
Sex-workers based in Bars	71.4	28.6	0	14.3	0	0	0	14.3
Equal-share Sex-workers	40	60	0	0	0	0	20	40
Sex-workers based in Drinking Places	50	50	0	0	0	0	0	50

The data on childhood upbringing attests that a significant majority
of my respondents (59%) were not raised by both of their biological
parents. Of these, those who were raised by single parents accounted for
31% of the sample, whereas those who were raised by other relatives
added up to 13%. The remaining 9% were raised by their grandparents,
whereas 5% were raised by a combination of one biological parent and a
stepparent, and 1% by a stepparent only. The data on the material
condition of the households in which the women grew up yielded an
interesting result. Whereas 51% came from households that they
described as poor or very poor, 43% came from "self-sufficient"
households. An interesting 6% came from "well-to-do" or "very rich"
households.

Slightly under a quarter of Addis Ababa's sex workers (24%) have
had no schooling at all. The majority (about 46%) had some kind of
elementary education, i.e. below or up to the sixth grade. An interesting

18% are women who have some kind of secondary education, and of these 11% had actually completed high school! There appears to be an equally interesting phenomenon of sex workers going to school part time. 2% of the women in my sample were currently attending classes, 1% at the elementary level, and 1% at the secondary level.

TABLE IV

Cross Tabulation of Level of Formal Education of Sex Workers and Categories of Sex- Workers (As Percent of Total within Each Category)

Categories of sex - workers	No Education	Basic Literacy	Completed Elementary	Discontinued Elementary	Completed Secondary	Discontinued Secondary
Fixed-share Sex-workers	42.9	0	0	48.6	2.9	5.7
Asphalt Sex-workers	0	0	0	48	20	24
Independent Home-based Sex-Workers	41.7	0	0	41.7	0	16.7
Sex-workers based in Hotels and Nightclubs	0	0	9.1	54.5	9.1	27.3
Sex-workers based in Bars	14.3	0	0	28.6	42.8	14.3
Equal-share Sex-workers	40	0	0	40	0	20
Sex-workers based in Drinking Places	25	0	0	25	25	25

Another interesting fact regarding education and commercial sex relates to the stated reasons for dropping out of school. Overall, 63% of my informants are school dropouts. Of these, a substantial 88% said that they left school for "lack of financial or other kinds of support". Only 6.3% said that they left because they were disinterested in school while 3.3% gave as a reason unavailability of schools nearby.

3.4 Stated Reasons for Entry into Sex-work

Under this variable, what I wanted to explore was the factors that actually pushed or pulled Addis Ababa's sex workers into this line of work. My overall objective is, of course, to learn how and to what extent the manner in which women become sex workers affects the way they relate to other people in various categories. However, there are other equally important considerations also. One of these, for instance, is exploring the differences that might actually exist between basic or fundamental causes that push women toward sex work and the immediate reasons that lie behind the decision of individual women to take up the work. The former are general and relate to commercial sex only indirectly, whereas the latter are specific and relate to the institution directly.

Not all women who are poor and uneducated become sex workers. Nor do all women who come from broken families or broken marriages, or who are migrants to the city, end up in commercial sex work. In fact, there are also women who come from fairly well to do and even wealthy families who end up in commercial sex work. Likewise, many women who end up in sex work, as well as their parents, had fairly high levels of education. There are also many who come from two parent families that raised them with material comfort and good care. Many women are taking up the work while still living with their families. The collection and interpretation of data on the immediate factors that led women to become sex workers is important, therefore, to disentangle the basic causes from the immediate reasons and to see what combinations of both factors account for most of the cases. This endeavor is also guided by the belief that interventions to prevent the entry into commercial sex of an ever increasing number of young women have to be made at two different levels, one addressing the basic causes and the other addressing the precipitating circumstances.

It is also important to study precipitating reasons because these reasons relate to the type of sex work that the women take up, to the degree to which they accept it as their station in life, to the overall mental frame with which they practice the trade and to their future plans and aspirations. For instance, a woman who had run away from home and started commercial sex by way of protesting against harsh discipline might consider the work as a temporary means of staying away rather than as a permanent source of livelihood. Such a woman might, in fact, hesitate to identify herself as sex-worker as such, and might as a result not subject herself to many of the rules of the game. Likewise, a woman who started working to earn a little more cash to supplement her income from another job or who moved into sex work to finance the purchase of expensive clothing or jewelry that she has seen on other women might even deny that she is a sex worker. In contrast, a woman who took up commercial sex in order to feed her starving family or to keep her orphaned siblings in school might consider her act as an act of sacrifice and might accept her situation and proceed with all the necessary precautions.

My findings affirm that there is, indeed, a distinction between basic causes and immediate reasons but that the two are related in many ways. The basic causes are stated when the women are asked *why* they became sex workers whereas the precipitating reasons are stated in response to the more direct question of *how* they became sex workers. For the women in my sample, the list of basic causes is made up of two major elements. They are running away from economic problems at home (63%) and a lure away from home by a relative or friend (21%). Less significant but frequently mentioned causes (accounting for 10%) are disagreement with or abuse by family members (mostly for city-born women), and attractions of the city and its amenities like education (rural-born women) (3%). Over 80 percent of the respondents who accounted for their becoming sex workers in terms of lure were of rural origin. Similarly, over 80% of those who said that they were forced into it by poverty or other social problems are of urban origin. Those who attributed their turn to sex work due to rural socio-economic problems (like broken marriage, famine, civil disturbances, etc) were not more than 20% of that category. Likewise, those who attributed their decision to enter commercial sex to urban social problems (not related to economic problems) were not more than 20%. The numerical data as well as the interviews strongly suggest that commercial sex is fed from within the city by primarily economic problems and from outside of the city primarily by extra-economic problems.

The responses to the question of *how*, actually, the women turn to commercial sex, however, brings out another set of factors, which, at least at first sight, appear to have a degree of relative independence from the basic causes. 53% of the respondents in my sample said that they became sex workers because they were unable to find another job. A significant 20 % said that they followed the example of a friend. An interesting 20% also said that they came into it unknowingly, apparently manipulated by other people (the chief culprits are the procurers known as d§§ (*delala*) and elderly women who become their first employers). 7% said that they started it casually and unintentionally, one thing leading to another. However, it appears that most women give these reasons by way of avoiding questions about their sexual morality that they believe would follow if they were to admit that they turned to sex business as the better of the alternatives that they had available to them.

This emerges clearly from the fact that most of the women (61%) had actually tried some other kind of work before taking up commercial sex work and they speak openly about the constraints and problems associated with those types of work in contrast to sex work. 18% of these women had done private work; 44.2% had worked as domestics; 34.4% had worked in small business establishments like restaurants and laundries. What is interesting is that out of these women over 85 % of them said that sex work was better paying than the types of work they were doing before. Only 13% said that it was actually less paying and 1.5% said that there was no difference. Equally significantly, the women also rated sex work very favorably in terms of independence. Nearly 90% said that sex work brought them more independence than the kinds of work that they did before, and enabled them to have better control over their lives. Only 13% said that sex work was actually more constraining and about 5% said there was no difference in this regard.

Both the numerical data and the interview material suggest to me that most women enter commercial sex both by way of running away from problems and to improve their conditions, both materially and socially. They run away from economic deprivation and at the same time seek to improve their economic lot. Likewise, they run away from forms of social control that they find intolerable, and they find in commercial sex a room in which they can make their own decisions. However, irrespective of whether the women were in fact compelled or lured into commercial sex, what they believe to be the reason for coming into the job is very important. It is very important because it has significant explanatory value for how the women behave socially.

3.5   Social Ties and Obligations

I use the phrase "social ties" to refer to relationships between the sex worker and other people toward whom the woman feels that she has an obligation or that they have an obligation towards her. These relationships could be between the woman and her family members or between her and other close kin or friends. The obligations could have been incurred prior to involvement in commercial sex or after. What is particular about social ties, as opposed to social relationships of other kind, is that they tend to be structural rather than voluntary or willful. A relationship between a sex worker on the one hand, and her parents, siblings, children or spouse on the other, are even more structural in the sense that they are developed in the context of the institutions of family and marriage. Social ties between the woman and these categories of people tend to be strong and the obligations owed to them or claimed from them would tend to be taken as natural in her eyes. The social ties between the woman and other relatives, kin or friends are less structured and less likely to be taken as natural, but can be cultivated and built into strong ties in which the woman is either expected to give or expects to receive support in material or emotional terms.

Social ties are, therefore, ties in which relationships of dependence exist, irrespective of whether the dependence means that it is other people who make claims on the woman's money and/or time or that it is the woman who makes claims on other people's money and/or time. What is distinctive about social ties in this sense is that the giver gives and the receiver receives the resources without expecting a return in any immediate sense. It could be a one-way flow, and not, therefore, necessarily a transaction. This definition of social ties excludes all other forms of social relationship that the woman may engage in: relationships that are short term or casual or relationships that involve give-and-take (transactions). Such, for instance, are relationships between the woman and other co-workers, acquaintances, neighbors, distant kinsmen or co-members in associations like *iqub* or *idir*.

The significance of this variable for a comprehensive differentiation of sex workers is that it has, like the other four variables, a degree of independence from the type of sex work that the women do. A woman who has poor parents or siblings to support or children of her own to take care of would behave differently from another one who does not have such ties of dependence even if the two women did the same kind of sex work.

Contrary to common assumptions that the sex worker is a woman who is socially dead, a closer look at the women who practice the trade in Addis Ababa shows clearly that many of them, in fact, are very much alive socially. One of the conditions dictating this social engagement is the fact that entrance to commercial sex work does not necessarily and invariably entail severance of social ties that the women had developed prior to their becoming sex workers. The other is that work in commercial sex does not necessarily and invariably prevent the development of new social ties between the women and a host of other people. Owing to these two facts, the average sex worker in Addis Ababa is a woman who is either struggling to maintain old ties or to build and sustain new ones. The Western idea of "a prostitute" who is all by herself and works and lives for herself alone is, therefore, more the exception than the rule in Addis Ababa.

TABLE V

Contact with Family Members and With Kin of Commercial Sex Workers in Each Category (As Percent of Total within Each Category)

Categories of sex workers	Contact with family members				Contact with kin			
	Yes	No	With some only	Don't have any family	Yes	No	With some only	Don't have any kin
Fixed-share Sex-workers	68.6	28.6	2.9	0	60	37	2.9	0
Asphalt Sex-workers	76	20	0	4	40	60	0	0
Independent Home-based Sex-Workers	83.3	16.7	0	0	83.3	16.7	0	0
Sex-workers based in Hotels and Nightclubs	63.6	18.2	9.1	9.1	45.4	45.4	9.1	0
Sex-workers based in Bars	85.7	14.3	0	0	57.1	42.8	0	0
Equal-share Sex-workers	60	40	0	0	60	40	0	0
Sex-workers based in Drinking Places	100	0	0	0	75	25	0	0

The data on social ties maintained by sex workers comes from responses to questions that I posed to the women about parents, siblings and children and the ways in which they relate to them. A significant 74% of the women in my sample stated that they maintain some kind of contact with their family members. Only 22% said they do not. 2% said that they maintain contact with some selected members of their family. 2% said that they had nobody they call family. Even more interesting is the data on the dependence of close members of family on the women. 38% of the respondents said that there are people among their family members who are currently fully dependent on their income from commercial sex. In terms of actual numbers, 63% of these had one person who is fully dependent on them; 18.4% take care of two persons, 7.8% maintain 3 persons, 2.6% maintain four and another 7.8% carry the full weight of

71

more than five persons.   71% of these dependents, constituting the absolute majority, are the children of the women themselves. Next come parents and siblings, each of which constituted 21% of the dependent population. 7.8 % of them were made up of other close relatives.

It is remarkable that 78.9% of the women who have fulltime dependents live with their dependents under the same roof; 21% support dependents who live elsewhere in the city while 15.7% maintain their dependents who live elsewhere in the country. All but one of the respondents who maintain fulltime dependents said that they provide support because the dependents do not have anybody else to support them. Another interesting fact regarding this dependence on commercial sex work is that in most cases the support is long term, having lasted at the time of the survey for an average of five years and above.

The figures on partial dependence of other people on the proceeds of commercial sex are even stronger. 46% of my respondents said that they support one or more individuals partially. Among them 56% support one person, 13% support two persons, 8.6% support three, 6.5% support four and a remarkable 23.9% support more than five people. These recipients of partial support include grandparents (4.3% of the cases), parents (73.9%), siblings and half-siblings (50%), children (17.3%), other close relatives (2.1%) and even in-laws (2.1%). Of the women who provide this partial support for dependents, 17.3% provide the support by housing the dependents with them, 41.3% support them within the city, 54% support them at a distance in another part of the country. The partial support that the women give to these categories of dependents is in most cases given "fairly regularly" (76%). Only rarely (in 28% of the cases) was support given "once in a while" and even more rarely (2.1%) was it given at fixed intervals and occasionally. As in the case of full support, the partial support being given by sex workers to partial dependents has run on the average for five years and above at the time of the survey.

Sex workers are also recipients of support from others.   20% of respondents in my sample said that they had in the past, or do currently, receive support from people with whom they have social ties. In 75% of the cases, this support comes from men who are lovers (55%), from men who have fathered their children (20%) and from female friends (5%). But there are also relatives who provide support for 15% of them. A curious 10% said that they get support from their spouses.   5% of the women who get this support also live with the supporters, 60% of them get the support

TABLE VI

Full or Partial Dependents on Commercial Sex Workers in Each Category
of Sex workers (As percent of total within each category)

Categories of sex workers	Fully Dependent		Partially Dependent	
	Yes	No	Yes	No
Fixed-share Sex-workers	31.4	68.6	57.1	42.9
Asphalt Sex-workers	48	52	16	84
Independent Home-based Sex-Workers	33.3	66.7	58.3	41.7
Sex-workers based in Hotels and Nightclubs	36.4	63.6	45.4	54.5
Sex-workers based in Bars	14.3	85.7	85.7	14.3
Equal-share Sex-workers	40	60	40	60
Sex-workers based in Drinking Places	100	0	100	0

from within the city. An interesting 35% said that they get the support
from relatives abroad who send them remittances or from people whose
residences they are not sure about. At the time of the survey the average
number of years that these women have been receiving this support was
roughly 3 years.

4   Conclusion

The general data that I presented in this chapter shows in part that the
morphology of commercial sex in Addis Ababa has undergone some
significant changes since it was studied by social scientists like Laketch
and Andargatchew in the 1970s and 1980s. In part, however, what the
data show is a picture that emerges from a perspective that seeks to
illuminate the social basis of the institution. In any case the following set
of tentative observations can be made about the situation of commercial
sex in Addis Ababa.

Sex-workers in Addis Ababa are typically very young women who
began work actually as children. Most are born and brought up here in
Addis. Women in this category are typically never married. Typically,

73

again they are relatively better educated. Most have troubled family backgrounds, characterized both by breakup of family and severe economic deprivation. However, sex workers of rural origin constitute a significant minority in the sex-worker population of the city. They are as young as those who originated here in the city. They are still relatively less educated, and a significant number are illiterate. Most of them came to the city in anticipation of better life, not necessarily to escape economic misery or due to social dislocation.

There are two important observations that can also be made about commercial sex workers in Addis Ababa, both of them significant for an analysis of the social context of their lives. One is that the overwhelming majority of the women live where they work and under conditions in which the living and working quarters are not separated. Most live either in very crowded conditions or semi-nomadically with frequent shifts in the venue of work. The other observation is that the majority of Addis Ababa's sex workers are women who maintain ties with a wide variety of people ranging from family members to other relatives and kin. Most of them are women who have dependents and a good number of them also depend on others. As a result they sustain a number of other people on their income from sex work as they are sustained in sex work partly with the help of those people. It is clear, however, that the women sustain more than they are sustained by others.

The above observations, however, are not only tentative but also very general. Both commercial sex and sex workers present a highly varied picture when looked at from a closer range. Their social connections and their social commitments are likewise highly varied. I will deal with this level of variety in the next chapter.

Chapter Four

Negotiating Physical Space: Work, Residence and Sex Work
in Addis Ababa

In this chapter I will take the scheme that I presented in the last chapter one level down and provide major highlights of the different types of sex work in Addis Ababa and the conditions of work and residence associated with each. I will also provide relevant data on the profiles of women who operate under each category.

I have three objectives in this chapter. One is to show that each type of sex work is associated with a distinct profile of the women who function in it and with distinct ways in which work and residence are organized under it. The second is to show that the way the women get access to venues of work and residence has determined their relationship with other people who have control over these venues. In this connection, I will argue that the serious problem of housing in Addis Ababa has forced sex workers to negotiate terms of access to physical space that are very harsh and exploitative. The third objective is to present data that I hope will show that certain types of commercial sex have been growing and expanding while others have been shrinking or declining. Such documentation will set the framework for my discussion, in the next chapter, of the ways in which sex work is socially embedded.

The volume of material that I will present in this chapter will be somewhat unequally distributed among the various types of sex work. Relatively detailed material will be provided for three types: fixed-share sex work, asphalt sex work and sex work done out of bars. Relatively less material will be provided on the remaining four types: sex work based on fifty-fifty share, sex work done independently out of residential houses, sex work done out of small drinking places and sex work done out of big hotels and night clubs. This imbalance results from one major factor, and that is that each type of sex work in the second group exhibits interesting parallels and similarities with one or another type in the first group regarding both the organization of work and residence and the profile of the women who engage in it. These similarities are in some cases considerable, although not so overwhelming as to invalidate the separation of the types as types. I thought, therefore, that to restate the points on which there are parallels and similarities would be redundant.

What I will do, instead, is to focus on the points of difference in my discussions of the types in the second group. The unequal volume and the sequencing of the material will show which of the types in the second group share parallels and similarities with which of the types in the first group.

I will organize the discussion under each type of sex work around "venues and conditions of work", "household and domesticity" and "profiles". "Venues and conditions of work" refers to the places where (or out of which) the women work and the terms and conditions that apply to the women who do work there. "Household and domesticity" refers to the ways in which the women live, household referring to the arrangements regarding the material side of residence (rental arrangements, food, furniture, etc) and domesticity referring to the social side of residence (the presence or absence of conjugal, parental or affective ties between the women and other people who may reside with them). "Profiles" will highlight the chief characteristics of the women in each category and will portray the "typical" woman on the basis of the characteristics shared by most women in the category.

1 The *Akafay*: Sex Work for Fixed Share and the Women Behind it

1.1 Venues and Conditions of Work

This category of work takes place in the residences of the women. The houses in which the women work are "owned" by other individuals, who are almost always women. These women, to whom we can refer as "madams", would have in turn either rented the houses from the *qabale* or from individuals to whom the *qabale* has rented out the houses. The "ownership" of the house by the madam is symbolized by the bed, which she purchases and makes available for the job. The houses in which this work is carried out are generally single-room structures, often so tiny that little else is accommodated besides the bed and a couple of chairs. In many of the houses that I visited, there is no separation of residential space from workspace. Most rudimentary types of household utensils are either hung on the walls or stowed away under the beds. In some of the houses, some kind of liquor trade goes on, often involving local drinks like *araqi* and *tella*.

The kiosk-type "houses" in which this category of sex work takes place are located in some of the worst slums of Addis Ababa. The ones that I have visited are located in Charqos (immediately to the south and west of the railway terminal), behind Maskal Square (where *Katanga*, the most famous of them is located), in the Kolfe area, in Arat Kilo (the neighborhood behind the Ministry of Education and Tourist Hotel) and in the Piazza area (in front of the Hagar-Fikir Theatre). Even though I am not certain, my tentative impression is that these slums grew out of early settlements of sex workers surrounding military camps or working class concentrations. In any case, one of the most defining characteristics of the kiosks in which this kind of operation takes place is that they are all gathered together in settlements. The structures are not only crowded together but also generally run-down and separated one from the other by cardboard or rusty iron sheets. The neighborhoods are generally known for the sex business, but also sell night accommodation for the cheapest prices.

The women in the kiosks may solicit by standing in front of their rooms for long hours. Sometimes they stand into the wee hours of the morning. Their activities are in most cases closely monitored by the madams for whom they work. The latter generally live in the same neighborhood, oftentimes right next door or behind a partition in the same house; they would, therefore, be within "eye-shot" of the sex house. There are cases, however, where the "madams" do not live in the neighborhoods. In such cases, the system operates either on trust or through representatives who monitor the activities of the *akafay*.

The fixed-share system works on the principle that the woman puts away a fixed amount of money for the madam every time that she entertains a man. The rates vary from place to place and from person to person. Collection is made either on a daily or a weekly basis and sometimes irregularly. If the arrangement between worker and madam is not based on trust, the regime of control and coercion could be very harsh indeed. The nature of control depends also on whether or not the madam is an entrepreneur who has several sex workers under her. A woman who has many workers can afford to relax the conditions of work and even hope to build affective ties with her workers. In fact, some of the long-standing fixed-share sex workers have developed such affective ties with their madams, referring to them as their "mothers". "Mothers" who handle their "daughters" carefully would not make a fuss over the share that they are paid; they would be less strict on hours of work or on the length of sessions. Some might even allow their "children" to take breaks or sleep off a sickness or boredom. A "mother" would also tend to be lenient and "generous" if her "worker" is "hot" and attracts clients better than others in the neighborhood.

More often than not, however, the madams themselves would be former sex workers whose best days are behind them and who find themselves in financial straits. The fact that they are well versed with the rates and techniques of sex work means that they have managerial expertise which they can put to good use. Some of them insist that the women stand for as long as they possibly can. To encourage these nocturnal vigils, my informants say, the madams often compel the women to chew *chat* during the day or consume stimulants like coffee in large quantities.

From what informants who work in this line of sex work say, it is clear that the lot of the women varies from madam to madam. In the words of one of my informants, a voracious and mean woman "will even try to have you sleep with anybody under any condition as long as the person pays money". There were times, according to my informants, when the "mothers" would be disappointed if a negotiation between her "child" and a client fails. "There are women who would want to hang you if you said no to a man even if that was because the man asked for sex without a condom", says one of my informants. That is what partly explains the fact that the most serious and (in fact the only) major source of insecurity for women in this category is contracting diseases. All the 35 respondents said that they fear that they might contract sexually transmitted diseases any time.

One of the major characteristics of the fixed-share system is a relatively high turnover of the women. Women move in and out of these arrangements in part because they are harsh regimes that cannot be tolerated but mainly because the madams themselves would want to replenish their supply before income from a worker starts to decline because she becomes less attractive. Despite the turnover in terms of changing madams, however, the tendency for the women to stay within the same line of work is very high. Out of my 35 respondents who are engaged in this type of sex work, 5 (14.2%) have been doing this work for as long as 5-10 years. 20% have been working for 3-4 years and another 20% for 2-3 years. What many of my informants consider being an improvement in their lives is that a fixed share system is better than a fifty-fifty share with which many of them will have started out.

Payment for sexual services under this system varies from place to place and depends on the type of service that is given. It is, however, generally on the low side. In fact there are many women who said to me that they accept whatever is offered. However, the overall range is between 5-10 *birr* for short sessions (called *short*) and 15 to 20 *birr* for overnight service (called *adar*).

1.2 Household and Domesticity

Work and residence are combined in this type of sex work. The women do not pay rent for their place of residence because it is also the place of their work. However, it is unlikely for a woman who works on a fixed-share basis to set up a household or to accommodate other people in the kiosk. For this reason, women who have children or other dependents tend to support them elsewhere rather than in residence with them. There are, however, many who do so. 25.7% of my respondents from this category (i.e. out of a total of 35 women) said that their dependents (mostly their children) live with them.

There are also cases in which space is shared between the *akafay* and the madam. When this happens, the living quarters of the two women will usually be separated by a curtain. In very rare cases, the madam may have a child, a spouse or a relative who lives with her so that more than two persons may be living in rooms that are sometimes as little as 4 meters by 4 meters.

1.3 Profiles

This is by far the most widespread form of commercial sex work in Addis Ababa today. 35% of the women in my sample are engaged in this type of sex work. Migrant women are heavily represented in this type, comprising 69% of the workers. 17% of the women arrived in Addis Ababa within the last two years. 14.3% have been in town for 3-5 years. Over 57% of all the respondents have been in Addis for less than 10 years. 40% of all the women in this category were born and brought up in rural areas.

The women who work in this category are also the youngest of sex workers in my entire sample. The average age for the category is 21 years.

At entry into the job, 17% of the women were actually children below 15 years of age. 66% were teenagers between 16 and 20. 43% of the women in this category did not have a single day of schooling. Close to 50% had discontinued from elementary school. Only 3% had completed secondary school while 6% are secondary school dropouts.

The majority of the women in this category explained their entry into the job as a result of manipulation by other people. 40% of the women said that they were brought to the houses of the madams to do household work and were encouraged to stay on reluctantly. 22.8% said that they followed the example of a friend who did this kind of work before. 28.5% took it up because they were unable to find another job. Interestingly, however, 77.1% of the women in this category were previously engaged in another kind of work and 62.8% of them reported that commercial sex was better-paying than the jobs they did before.

69% of the women who do this kind of commercial sex maintain contact with their family members and close relatives. 45.7% have children, 25.7% of them having had the children since they started work. There is an interesting case of one respondent who is married and who does this kind of job with the full knowledge of her husband. 31.4% of the women in this category reported that they have persons who are fully dependent on their income from this work. 25.7% of them support one person fully; 9.09% supported two persons and another 9.09% supported over five persons fully. In 76.9% of the cases these dependents consisted of children; in 15.3% of the cases they were siblings of the women and in 7.69% of the cases they were their parents. In response to a question as to what they spend most of their earnings on, 37.1% of the respondents said "supporting dependents". Most of them (54.2%) said that they spend most of their earnings on food.

In summary, the typical woman who works as an *akafay* on a fixed-share basis is a completely unlettered young woman of about 21 who is a recent migrant to Addis Ababa. She had tried to work in domestic service at least once before she took up work in this area and was led into this line of work by procurers to whom she had gone to ask for work. She has a child whom she supports alone, but cannot keep the child with her due to the nature of her work.

2 Sex-work on Equal-Share

2.1 Venues and Conditions of Work

The venues in which this category of sex work is practiced are the same as those I described above for fixed-rate share work. Only the conditions of work differ. Under this variety, the sex worker basically hands over half of her earnings to the madam. This condition makes the relationship between the woman and the madam not only highly exploitative but also potentially unstable. Because the madam anticipates half of the earnings of the woman, she would have an even more compelling reason to keep the woman at work. She would be less disposed to allow her worker to spend time on other matters like socialization. In contrast to the madam who collects a fixed sum per session, the madam in this type of work would have a greater motivation to keep the woman on her feet, soliciting for long hours. She would also be disposed to encourage her to take whatever offers are made to her by clients.

These interests of the madam dictate that she employs one of two possible strategies: one is to impose the strictest control and highly invasive monitoring. This strategy includes being around the woman for most of the day and a little bit of investment in stimulants like coffee and *chat*. The other is to develop the highest possible level of affective ties with the woman so as to make her feel that she is actually working for her loving "mother". Depending on which of these two strategies the madams follow, the relationship between them and the women could be stable or unstable. It appears that where the madams adopt severe monitoring as a strategy, the women tend to get fed up quickly and look for a way out. The lucky ones and those who have saved some money might rent a room somewhere in the neighborhood and set themselves up as independent operators. Those that are no so lucky leave simply in the hope of finding another more "motherly" madam. Where the madams adopt the affective strategy, the women tend to stay put.

This difference was starkly demonstrated to me in the focus group discussion that I had with the women who do this kind of share work. Only one or two of the women in the discussion complained about life with their madams. The majority was highly appreciative of the madams and talked at length about the various things that they did for them. One of the things mentioned by one of the women was that her "mother" takes

81

care of her child. If it were not for the clues suggested by the discussions and the information from other categories of women who had done this kind of share work before, the figures from the survey data about the stability of this arrangement would have been very difficult to understand. In the data, some 40% of the respondents from this category said that they have been doing this work for 5 to 10 years! Another 40% said that they have been doing it for 3 to 4 years. This is a remarkably high rate of stability. The focus group discussions and the interviews with former equal share *akafay* explained to me that due to the very high turnover induced by the exploitative and unstable nature of this arrangement the pool of respondents is likely to be made up of women who are stuck to it through the strategy of affection.

Remuneration for sexual services in this category of work is broadly similar to that of the fixed-share arrangement. For short sessions, women are paid generally from 3 to 10 *birr*; for overnight sessions they charge anywhere between 15 and 20 *birr*. Many women who work in this category are so desperate that they might take even lesser offers.

2.2 Household and Domesticity

There is no observable structural difference between the living conditions of this category of women and those in the fixed-rate share work described above. From the interviews with women in this category it turns out that most of them actually live with their madams in the same room or quarters, separated one from another by curtains or material like cardboard. The women share food and other material with their "mothers". The affective strategy, it appears, dictates this arrangement of household. There are also cases where the women are allowed to live along with their dependents. 20% of my respondents in this category actually said that they have a dependent who lives with them. This dependent is usually a child. As stated above, the fact that their children are allowed to live with them makes the women in this category to be especially indebted to their "mothers".

2.3 Profiles

This category accounts for a relatively small percentage of Addis Ababa's sex workers. It constitutes only 5% of my general sample. The majority of them (60%) are migrant women. Interestingly, however, they have been in town for relatively long periods of time. 40% said that they have been in Addis for over 10 years, while all the rest have been in town for at least 7 years.

The women in this category are fairly older than the average sex worker in town. The average age for the category is 24 years. Age of entry, likewise, is slightly higher for this group than for others. 40% started work between 16 and 20 while 60% started somewhere between 21 and 25. 40% of the women in this category did not go to school at all, whereas another 40% had dropped out of elementary school. 20% had started but did not finish high school.

80% of the women in this group said that they became sex workers because they were unable to find another job. 20% said that they followed in the footsteps of a friend. However, all of the women interviewed said that they had done other kinds of work prior to coming to sex work and 80% of them say that sex work is better paying and 60% say that it gives more freedom. The work that the majority (6%) did previously was domestic work. 60% of the women in this category maintain contact with their folks while 40% do not. None of their folks know, however, what they do for livelihood. 40% have dependents, for 20% of them the dependents consisted of parents while for the remaining 20% they consisted of children.

The typical equal-sharing *akafay* seems to be a woman in her mid to late 20s, migrant and uneducated. She appears to be the type who has stayed in a difficult and exploitative form of sex work for many years and appears resigned to it.

3   Independent Home-based Sex-work and the Women Behind it

3.1   Venues and Conditions of Work

Externally, the structures from which women in this category do work are not very different from the *akafay* women described above. Indeed many of these women are neighbors and friends of women who work as *akafay*. There are, however, major differences in the conditions of work and the consequent arrangement of residence and workspace.

The independent sex worker works in a house that she has rented either from the *qabale* or from another person to whom the *qabale* has rented the house. She is, therefore, in total control of the circumstances under which she does her work. Her independence is symbolized by her ownership of the bed; hence the designation ባለ፡አልጋ *(bale-alga)*. She budgets her time and her energy at work and has full control over her income. The houses that I have visited varied in size as well as in their internal organization. Some were fairly spacious and relatively well furnished. Others were awfully small and very poorly furnished. Most of the tiny ones are spaces rented from other tenants.

There are a few cases of women in this category who operate from locations that are a little removed from concentrated settlements of sex workers. I observed that these women tended to be less free about their movements and about the movements of clients. Otherwise, this category of sex workers appears to be the most settled in the profession and the most experienced. They feel relatively more secure both in terms of their physical safety and other job-related matters, like disease contraction.

Overall, the independent operator may be said to be a woman who is on her way to be a madam some day. Her biggest asset is that she is in control of the house in which she lives and works. One of my informants in this category in fact runs a full household, complete with a husband at home.

Remuneration for sexual services by women in this category is not very different from the two categories discussed above, but there is slightly wider variation. Short sessions are charged from 10 to 20 *birr* while overnight services cost anywhere between 15 and 30 *birr*. The most important difference in this case, of course, is that the women get to keep all their earnings.

3.2 Household and Domesticity

It might be possible to speak in terms of two subcategories of women in this category, based primarily on the way domestic arrangements are intertwined with residence and work. One subcategory consists of women who have rented the house from the *qabale* themselves and have no children or other dependents living with them. The other subcategory consists of women who have sub-rented the house from other individuals and have children or other dependents living with them. 25% of the women in my sample have rented the house in which they live and work from the *qabale* directly. Another 25% have rented the house from a person who owns the house. The remaining 50% have sub-rented the house from people who have rented it from the *qabale*. The first group of women pays relatively little in terms of house rent, although utilities may be a headache if customers are not forthcoming. For the latter two groups, rent constitutes a big headache because renting even a tiny room from individuals, be they owners or themselves tenants, costs a lot of money. When dependents are added to a house rented from individuals further complications inevitably arise. For one thing the woman may not be able to work on a flexible schedule. Consequently, her income suffers. For another, dependents become a drain on what is left.

One of the mechanisms through which women who have a little space try to overcome their dire financial circumstances is by setting up one or two beds in the house (as space permits) to rent to overnight users. What results is an incredible efficiency of room use in which two or three people who do not know each other might spend a night in a tiny room. On one side of the room would sleep a person who had rented a bed for a night; in another corner the woman might be sleeping with a client. Still in another corner (if possible fenced off by some cloth or cardboard) a child or children might be sleeping.

3.3 Profiles

This category consists of the third largest category of Addis Ababa's sex worker population, next to the fixed-rate *akafay* and the asphalt workers that will be discussed below. A significant 67% of the women are migrants to Addis. However, in contrast to all other categories of migrant sex workers of the city, they have been around for quite some time. 50% of them have been in Addis for over 10 years. In fact there are many women in this category who have been in town doing this work for nearly two decades or more. The shortest length of residence in Addis reported for this category is five years.

The women in this category are also the oldest in my entire sample. The average age of the women added up to 31 years. Starting age also was on the upper side for most of them. 25% started between the ages of 16 and 20. 33% started between 21 and 25. 17% were over 25 when they came into the job. 42% of the women in this category whom I surveyed had no schooling at all. Another 42% had discontinued before completing elementary school. Only 17% had started, but never completed, high school.

Like the other categories of sex workers, the majority of the women in this category also attributed their entry into commercial sex to failure or inability to find another job. 83% of them gave this explanation. Only 16% said that they followed a friend into the work. Yet, again like other categories of women, the majority of them also reported that they have done some other kind of work prior to coming to commercial sex. 66% reported this to be the case. 87% of these said that commercial sex is better paying than the work they had done before, most of which was domestic work. Most of the women in this category maintain contact with their folks. 83% reported this to be the case, although only 30% of these said that their folks knew what they were doing. A substantial 66% of these women have children. For 62.5% of them the children live with them. These women also support other people either fully or partially. 33% said that they have people who depend entirely on them, most of them children. 58% said that they support other people partially, most of them parents and siblings.

In summary, a typical independent operator is a middle-aged woman who has been in this line of work for quite some time. She is likely to be a migrant but with a long record of residence in the city. She is likely to be illiterate. Above all, the independent operator is a very experienced woman who is not very worried about when she would leave this line of work. Her worries are likely to be that of customers and money. She is also likely to be a head of a household in which at least another person lives.

4   Asphalt Sex-Work and the Women Behind It

4.1   Venues and Conditions of Work

Asphalt walkers concentrate in the downtown area of Addis Ababa, along the streets that radiate from the Maskal Square towards the southern and eastern parts of the city. These are also streets along which the major hotels and centers of night entertainment are located. As working venues, the different corners along these streets are staked out or "reserved" by different groups of sex workers as their respective "turf". Sometimes these turfs are jealously guarded and involve negotiations or even quarrels among established "owners" and newcomers. My informants say that they have a thorough and detailed knowledge of the streets on which they work; they know not only what exists where and what its relationship is to their work, but also who owns which establishment or who the key workers are in each establishment. They say that there are places along the streets that they use as resting, refreshment or eating places; there are places where they drop in to see if they could find clients.

Even more importantly, in the course of time the women succeed in converting some of the structures along the streets into structures that facilitate their work. The structures become their service providers, catering to their needs for supply as well as communication and security. For instance, my informants say that each group of sex workers utilizes one or more retail kiosks located along the streets both as supply station(s) for such items as cigarettes, gums, toilet paper, etc., and as points of gathering, dispersion and communication among themselves and with others. Kiosks that provide telephone services are particularly useful as nodal points. Over a period of time relationships between the kiosk owners and the women develop from a relationship of seller and buyer to a relationship of friendship that involves the exchange of goods, information and favors. The women take supplies from the shopkeepers on credit when they don't have cash on them, but also sometimes deposit with them jewelry (when they feel insecure about clients) or money that they collect by way of pre-payment for their services. The kiosk owners sometimes supply information to the women about their clients, particularly if the latter had been looking for them when they were not around, etc.

The most important structures that asphalt workers would like to have along the streets on which they work, or somewhere close-by, are hotel rooms. Hotels are places to which the women direct their clients for sexual services. For reasons that will be mentioned shortly, there are times when the women would be unwilling to go to any other venue with clients. It therefore becomes crucial for the women to be well acquainted both with the physical morphology of these hotels and the human element that operates them. Friendships are quickly struck between the women and hotel staff such as receptionists and guards. The friendships are cemented with exchanges of information, gifts and other resources. From this relationship both sides benefit.

In terms of conditions of work, asphalt workers say that their line of work is the most difficult and also the most dangerous of all forms of commercial sex work in the city. All the women in my sample of respondents from this category affirmed this point. They say that asphalt work is difficult because it involves staying out in the cold or in the rains for hours on end. Walking the streets or standing for hours are both boring and physically straining. They say that the wind and the cold take a toll on them, causing skin cracking and facial withering easily unless special precautions are taken. Both to stay awake and to weather the elements, the women regularly consume alcohol, cigarettes and stimulants like *chat*, often in very high quantities. Drugs, referred to by the women as "height", also come into the picture from time to time.

Asphalt women find themselves under constant harassment by the police. They describe their relationship particularly with the Federal Police as "one between a cat and a mouse". The police, they say, swoop on them sometimes, whisk them off the streets and subject them to all kinds of torment. They sometimes take them out of town and dump them in the wilderness where there is a real possibility of being carved up by hyenas. The most common form of punishment is being submerged in barrels containing ice-cold water. Work in the streets therefore involves constant alertness about the movements of the police, keeping track of their schedules and shifting points of operation to escape capture. The women's knowledge of the movements of the police is such that they clear from certain streets before the arrival of the police, sometimes returning after the latter have finished their scouting for the night. It is "a cat and mouse game" indeed.

The most defining characteristic of work in the streets, however, is the physical danger with which it is associated. The women say that they face great risks of being robbed, beaten, raped or otherwise abused by men, much more than all other categories of sex workers. They face these risks from all kinds of men, including from gangsters in the neighborhoods, but mostly from those who come to them as clients. Since the women are almost always picked up by motorists, they do not have full control over the terms of their engagement with clients. Although the women almost always insist that before entering vehicles there should be agreement with clients about amount of payment, venue of service and type of sexual service (i.e. whether it is short term or overnight service), very often the men tend to take control once the women are in their vehicles and movement begins. The men could take the women to unfamiliar places, to places so far off and out of the way that the latter are completely at their mercy. This exposes the women to all forms of abuse, including life-threatening situations. There have been many times, say the women, that women are gang-raped or forced to perform "strange" sex with men who have "strange" sexual preferences. It is common for women in this line of work to be robbed of their clothing, their jewelry or even the monies that they have received as pre-payment and to be left in the middle of nowhere in the complete darkness of early morning hours.

Despite a high-level of awareness among asphalt women about protected sex and the value of condoms, the inequality of power between these women and their clients is such that all their precautions could be useless. If they run into irresponsible men, as indeed they do frequently, their chances of being infected with HIV or other STDs are considerable. From time to time the women could find themselves in very unfortunate conditions indeed, conditions that could end up even in their murder. My informants say that some murders were committed in the most vicious and cruel manner by clients, including the cutting of the throats of the women.

The fact that working conditions for asphalt women are filled with strain and danger explains not only why the women need to be constantly alert, vigilant and aware of their surroundings as stated above, but also why streetwalking is the only form of sexual work linked to pimping in the sense in which this institution is known in the West. [1] Among the women in this category that I have interviewed, 16% had pimps. Pimps are men who are believed to provide protection to the women either through their connections with neighborhood gangs or in their own rights as neighborhood bullies. In return, they share their daily earnings. In fact, this "sharing" of the proceeds sometimes takes the form of men collecting all the earnings of the women and controlling subsequent expenditure. In some cases, the women take it as their primary mission to feed, clothe or otherwise satisfy "their men". Sexual services, of course, are part of the deal in a relationship between a pimp and his woman.

As in many parts of the world, pimping in Addis Ababa is also described in the language of love, emotional tie or conjugal relationship, not in the language of business partnership or sexual entrepreneurship.

---

[1] Incidentally, the literature on commercial sex in Ethiopia mistakenly refers to go-betweens or all those who convey information to and from sex workers as pimps.

Pimps are described by the women sometimes as their "[boy] friends", sometimes as their "lovers", sometimes even as their "husbands". This "special" and "intimate" relationship provides the context for the unrestricted and almost always unprotected sexual access that the men would have to the women. "Of course I don't use condoms with my friend", says Tigist, one of my informants, "although I worry sometimes who else he may be sleeping with, he remains to be my lover and is like my husband". Despite this language of love and intimacy, however, there is no doubt that the primary service of the pimps from the point of view of the women is that they guarantee them "respect" in the neighborhood where they work. In my discussions with them about this matter, many of my informants kept saying "ፍሬንዶ ያስከብረኛል!!" meaning, "my friend makes sure that I am respected". Of course, "respect" in this context refers to freedom from harassment by the other neighborhood thugs.

There are two distinctive characteristics of asphalt work that arise from the conditions associated with it. Both of these characteristics are also noteworthy in view of the arguments that I will put forward later about their socialization. One of them is that the women tend to spend a very high proportion of their incomes on clothing, shoes and cosmetics than all other categories of sex-workers. They explain this as investment required by the job itself. The other is that the women tend to be the most dependent of all sex workers on stimulants like alcohol, *chat* and cigarettes. In my sample of asphalt workers, over 90% said that they smoked, chewed *chat* or drank alcohol regularly. Work also requires investments in clothing

The remuneration that women who work on the asphalt get varies greatly, but generally it is on the upper side. Short-term sessions cost generally from 30 to 100 *birr*. Overnight service can bring in anywhere between 100 and 500 *birr*. The variation comes, according to the women, from the fact that they get good pay when they service expatriate clients or Ethiopians who are visiting from places such as America.

4.2 Household and Domesticity

Women that work on the asphalt tend to prefer to live together as roommates or to rent a house and live by themselves. 36 % of the women in my sample said that they lived with roommates who are their friends while another 36% said that they rented a house in which they live. 16%

said that they live with their parents and another 8% live with relatives who do not have a family. An interesting 4% of the women said that they don't have any fixed place of residence. Almost all of them work at some distance from their residence, not in the same neighborhood.

Asphalt women who live as roommates enter into various kinds of rental arrangements. The most common is a hostel-like arrangement in which a group of three or four women rent a single room and live there out of their suitcases. Typically, the women would have little or nothing by way of furniture or utensils in the house. There might or might not be any beds in the house. If beds do exist, it would most likely be a single one, to be used by all the roommates collectively. In those cases where no bed exists at all, the women would sleep on mattresses spread out on the floor. Because the women almost always eat outside, they do little or no cooking at home and thus own hardly anything by way of cooking ware.

Rental arrangements for these places vary considerably. Many of the places are actually partitioned spaces in houses or part-rooms in rooms occupied by other individuals or families. Typically, the landlord would be a person who might have himself rented the house from the *qabale*. In fact, the typical landlord would be a woman who supplements her income with such rentals. In some cases, the women pay rent to their landladies on a monthly basis. Often, however, rent is paid on a daily basis, as for hotel rooms, although the payment schedule is often flexible, as it should, in fact, be due to the irregularity of the women's income.

Still another arrangement of rental makes the place available to the women during the day and requires them to rent beds if they wanted to spend the night in the house. In some cases the women may be able to sleep on the floor if the bed or beds are rented out, but as a rule they cannot enter the house and sleep before the bed or beds are rented out.

There are three important characteristics of daily life in these hostel-type residences of asphalt women that are striking and interesting. One is related to the relationship among the women themselves; the second is related to the relationship between the women and their landladies; the third is related both to the relationship among the women and their relationship with their landladies.

The relationship among the women is characterized by "communalism" and arises from the nature of their work as well as the way they organize their households. Women who live together also work together. What this produces is a sense of being together in one situation, a sense reinforced by the belief that success and failure in the streets are a matter of chance rather than of any distinction. A woman who has done some "business" and has got some money today has to share it with roommates who did not succeed because she knows full well that she would be in their shoes tomorrow. The result is a life of communalism in which saving and long-term planning do not have much place. In the words of Selamawit, an asphalt worker, the motto guiding her and her friends is "let us share and eat and drink today; let us get the best clothing today; let us spend for satisfaction today; tomorrow will take care of itself".

The typical hostel-like residence of asphalt workers is, as I stated above, structured in such a way that the women and their landladies come into close and daily contact. These forces on both parties a relationship in which a lot more goes on than just payment and collection of rent. Interactions are intense and continuous around such issues as the use of utilities like electricity and water, the borrowing of household utensils, the comings and goings of people and security of property. However, how the two parties perceive this relationship varies from place to place and from person to person. The asphalt workers who addressed this issue in my focus group discussions tell different stories. Some say that their landladies are greedy and exploitative toward them because, in addition to the rent that they collect, they also expect other material benefits from them.

According to these informants, the women often helped themselves to their food, cigarettes or *chat* routinely, and expected occasional gifts from them in the form of domestic food supplies like bread, sugar and coffee beans. "Every time that we have done good business", one informant said: "they would look into our hands in the hope of getting something. Yet, if business is down and we failed to pay rent for some time, they start to behave funny towards us". Other informants disagree, saying that the women actually were social and "motherly"; they say that the women care for them very much and do not put pressure on them if they failed to do business and did not have rental money to pay. As with the *akafay* women that I discussed above, these differing representations of household by streetwalkers might reflect, at least in part, differing strategies that their landladies follow to make the most benefit out of their position as landladies. In other words, the landlady and the madam share a rather remarkable similarity in being described either as evil exploiters or as almost saintly mothers. It is quite possible, however, that the differences of opinion reflect the existence of both understanding and exploitative landladies.

The third element, the one that makes for complex relationships among the women as well as between them and their landladies, is the effort that the women make to accommodate "domestic" or intimate relationships with men in this already complicated arrangement. Very often this takes the form of trying to make pimps part of the domestic scene. From the stories that the women tell, it emerges that each woman who has a relationship with a pimp would try to steal a moment of privacy with her "lover" or "boyfriend" in such an unlikely place for privacy. Often things don't work, and involve costs for the women in the form of rentals for hotel rooms. This fact sometimes makes for a difficult relationship among the women as well as between them and their landladies.

In other arrangements of residence involving asphalt workers, what we see is a situation in which the women live either with their family or by themselves. Where they live by themselves, there may or may not be children or men living with them. In some cases, the women go out for sex work with the full knowledge of family members; in some, the women make efforts to "hide" the fact from them. In fact, what happens very often is that family members know what is going on but deliberately turn a blind eye. I will pick up this point later in the following chapter.

4.3 Profiles

"Asphalt-work" or work on the streets engages the second largest number of commercial sex workers in Addis Ababa today. In terms of the number of women involved it accounts for a quarter of the women in my sample. It is probably the most visible form of sex work in the city today and also the most rapidly expanding. Its visibility might have to do with the outdoor nature of the venue of work and with the fact that since the change of regime in the country in 1991, the very prohibitive measures against street solicitation existing previously have not been enforced. The rapidity of the expansion of this form of commercial sex, however, can be gleaned from my own sample. Some 64% of the women started work in the last four years, while 16% began in the last 2-3 years. A significant 24% came into the work within the last one-year period.

Most of the women who do this type of sex work are also indigenous to the city. 18 out of the 25 women who do this type of sex work (i.e. 72%) are born and brought up in Addis Ababa. The urban origin of the women is even more dramatically illustrated when we add to this figure those women who came to Addis from other urban areas. It comes to 92%.

The women in this category are also relatively young, only slightly older than the fixed-rate *akafay* women who make up the youngest category. The average age of asphalt women in my sample is 22. However, the disaggregated data on age is even more striking. About 16% of the women in the sample started sex-work as children below the age of 15 while 60% of them were teenagers at the point of entry.

The women who practice this kind of sex work are also the most educated of all the categories of sex workers except those working in small hotels or bars. Out of the 25 women in my sample, 12 (48%) had some elementary education but had dropped out before completing; 6 (24%) are high school dropouts, 5 (20%) have completed high school and 2 are still in school (1 in elementary and 1 in secondary school). An overwhelming majority of them (68%) say that they quit school because they did not have financial or other kinds of support.

Some 68% of the women in this category said that they became sex workers because they were unable to find another job. 12% attributed their engagement in sex work to peer influence, while another 12% claimed that they were lured into it unknowingly. For 8% sex work is something that they got into casually and unintentionally. My interviews with members of this last category established that many of them began sex work while in the process of "passing time" outside of their homes after quarreling with one or another parent, usually because the parent(s) did not approve of their romantic involvement with a boyfriend. Many, in fact, slid into sex work when the boys with whom they were infatuated abandoned them and they found themselves in limbo.

Another interesting point on which this category of women differs from others is the fact that few of them had done or had sought to do other work prior to taking up commercial sex. 60% said that they had never done any other work before, while the 40% who did do other work either had a job in a business establishment or did private work. None of them worked as a domestic, the line of work that most women in most of the other categories tended to engage in prior to turning to sex work. The women who did some other work were unanimous that sex work paid better than their previous work and an overwhelming 90% of these said that it also brought them more independence of action.

Over three-quarters of the women (76%) who work on the streets of Addis Ababa maintain contact with family members. Only 20% said they don't, while 4% said that they did not have any family. An interesting 50% of the women said that their family members knew directly or indirectly about their work. 32% percent of the women said that everybody in their family knows openly that they were sex workers, while 16% said that their family members knew what they did but not so openly. 48% of the women in this category carried the full weight of varying number of people with whom they have social ties. 28% supported one person, 12% supported 2 persons, 4% were bread earners for themselves and four other persons while another 4% maintain over five persons. For 28% of the women these dependents are children, for 12% they are parents, for 8% they are siblings and for 4% they are close relatives.

In summary, the typical streetwalker in Addis Ababa is a young woman in her early twenties who was born and brought up in the city. She is a person with at least elementary level education and might understand some English, even if she may not easily communicate in it. She is likely to be either a runaway from home because of a fallout with the family or a person forced out of the house by severe economic problems.

5   Hotel and Nightclub Sex Work and the Women Behind it

5.1 Venues and Conditions of Work

To a large extent, there is no difference between asphalt workers and women who go to hotels or nightclubs to look for clients. In fact, often they are the same people. Partly for this reason, as I have stated above, there is no individual sex worker or group of sex workers who identify themselves as hotel or nightclub sex workers. However, among the women in my sample who said that they combine different kinds of sex work, the majority of them worked between hotels and nightclubs, moving back and forth between the two. Some may not engage in asphalt work on a regular basis and might, in fact, operate from home. These elements justify a discussion of the women separately from the asphalt workers. A discussion of women who sell sex out of hotels and nightclubs is also justified because, in actual fact, these two venues are not always distinct and separate. They are structurally connected because all the major hotels in Addis also run nightclubs.

As stated above, the major hotels in Addis Ababa do not function as venues for sex workers in any official way. However, many of them house nightclubs to which a large number of sex workers come regularly. Many of these are fairly upper class sex workers who can afford to pay the entrance fees regularly and afford to pay for their own drinks. Many of my informants told me that these women seek to maintain an air of sophistication and pretend not to be sex workers. Many, in fact, could be office workers who engage in sex work part-time.

Both these women and women who cannot always afford the nightclubs operate from the hotels with some help and assistance from the hotel staff. The latter help the women to connect with clients through the phone. However, work sometimes involves a semi-regular drop-in by the women in the lobbies of the hotels as "guests", or of walking about in their parking lots or doorways. Most of the staff of the big hotels knows who these regular "guests" are, and often treat them as informal workers and refrain from hindering their movements. Many of the women who operate in this manner cater to expatriate clients and tend to be paid relatively high amounts. They are, therefore, relatively well off.

Besides the nightclubs in the big hotels, there are two different classes of nightclubs in Addis Ababa. One variety, which we can refer to as small clubs, are those in which live Ethiopian music is played by modern or traditional bands. These are often housed in small villas or roadside houses and cater mainly to Ethiopian clientele. There are no admission charges, except that one has to order drinks which tend to be twice or three times as expensive as in ordinary bars. The clubs where traditional music is played are known as አዝማሪ ቤት (*azmari bet*) and attract the least number of unattached women. Those clubs that play modern Ethiopian music have slightly greater attraction for women who may be looking for clients. However, even here, the tendency is still for young couples or for male youth to come together for entertainment rather than for unattached men coming to look for women. They are not therefore the usual targets for sex workers. The nightclubs that attract sex workers and their would-be clients are the big discotheques where DJ music is played. There are quite a few of these in Addis Ababa, generally in neighborhoods described above in connection with the asphalt sex workers. These night clubs are frequented by middle-aged and upper class type Ethiopians as well as foreigners.[2] Both of these types of men tend to be relatively more "liquid" and lonely than others. The clubs charge admission fees for sex workers in the amount of 20-30 *birr* per person. In addition to admission fees, the women would also be expected to order drinks. These expenses are sufficient to keep the lower-class type of street women away from the nightclubs. Once in on their own account, whatever the women do to help the club owners sell drinks would, of course, be appreciated by the latter. In fact, women who frequent the clubs and who accumulate this kind of credit with the club-owners would be admitted for several days for free. Birtukan, one of my informants, says that at the *Memo club*, the club to which she regularly goes, women would be allowed to enter for free after 2 months of entrance fee payment. There are places, like *The Concord Hotel*, where the women qualify for free admission after 6 months of good record. Women who could afford to be so regular and who prove helpful with the sale of drinks at the clubs eventually get into working relationships with the club staff some of whom help them with information about the comings and goings of their actual or potential clients.

Hotels naturally serve both as venues for meeting clients as well as for servicing them. Independent (non-hotel) nightclubs, on the other hand, do not generally have facilities for the provision of sexual services. Therefore, the women generally end up with clients in the hotel rooms to which they direct them. Some might also go to the residences of the clients.

Women who work between hotels and nightclubs have the same work-related insecurities that the asphalt workers have. The mechanisms they employ to deal with these insecurities are also generally similar. Remuneration, likewise, is generally the same. It is on the upper side, but characterized by high variation.

5.2 Household and Domesticity

There is a much greater chance for the women in this category to live by themselves or with family rather than with other sex workers as roommates. In fact, all of the women in my sample of this category said

---

[2] The women refer to the latter as ዜጋ (*zega*), short for የውጭ ዜጋ (ye-wuch zega) or foreigner.

that they lived with family or by themselves. It appears that this situation helps many of these women to maintain a certain degree of pretence that they are not full-time sex workers. That is because, in many cases, the relationships that the women build with foreigners out of the hotels and nightclubs lead to a situation in which they become "kept women", i.e. women supported and relatively well-maintained by their foreigner friends. When their foreigner friends are away, the women who have been generously remunerated by them move into a low-intensity mode of operation in sex work, going out for work only occasionally or when the need arises for money. Some of them might not need to come out at all, waiting only for the return of their businessman or diplomat friend to be replenished economically. The low-intensity mode into which they could afford to get periodically as well as their usually respectable financial standing thus makes it possible for many of these women to keep an image of self-supporting "clean" women rather than that of the sex worker.

5.3 Profiles

There is little or no difference in terms of profile between the asphalt workers and women in this category. They tend to be as young as the former and as relatively educated. They are predominantly urban in origin and are unlikely to have tried some other line of work prior to taking up sex work. Their reasons for becoming sex workers are also similar to those of the asphalt workers. However, their social ties appear to be slightly stronger than the asphalt workers. 64% of them maintain contact with their folks and 54% actually live with family. Interestingly however, an equal number (54%) said that their folks did not know what they did to earn money. It is also interesting to note that women in this category are more likely to be engaged in sexual relationships that they describe as non-commercial and not driven by the need for protection. 54% of the respondents said that they have boyfriends or lovers who did not start out as their clients. A small percentage (9%) of these men knew what the women did to get money but most did not know, at least not openly.

In short, the typical woman in this category is likely to be the relatively well- dressed and sophisticated-looking young woman of about 22 who is unemployed but as much as possible tries to maintain some degree of pretence that she is not a sex worker. She is relatively more independent than most other types of sex workers in the sense that she has neither a pimp nor a madam to subsidize. But she is no less of a bread-earner for dependents than others.

6 Sex Work out of Bars and the Women Behind it

6.1 Venues and Conditions of Work

Addis Ababa has hundreds of small hotels that combine the business of renting of hotel rooms with trade in a wide-range of beverages and liquors. Typically, waiting staff in the bars of these hotels are made up of women. Depending on its location and its size, a bar in a small hotel could have as few as five or as many as thirty women on its staff. Many would have even more. In some of the bars where some of my informants work there are more than fifty women who make themselves available for service every day. Ownership of small hotels and bars is not a gender-specific activity in Addis Ababa. The employers of the bar sex workers could be, therefore, both women and men.

The way the sex business works out of hotel bars, as well as the ways sex workers fit themselves into it, is determined by the work schedule of the bars. Bars are theoretically open from about 8:00 in the morning to mid-night or two o'clock. In actual fact, however, real business begins sometime in the late afternoon, around 4 or 5 o'clock, and warms up in the early evening. The peak hours are between 8:00 and 12:00 pm. This schedule makes it necessary both for the owners of the bars and the women who use the bars as venues for sex work to establish operational rules that allocate service and labor throughout the day and guarantee that both benefit from the peak hours during which most of their customers would be present.

Accordingly, each hotel-bar would typically have two subcategories of sex workers on its staff. One subcategory, known as አስተናጋጆች (waitresses) or የቤት፡ልጆች (children of the house), is made up of a small number of women who constitute the core staff of the establishment. These women are regarded as full-time employees of the hotel-bar and are paid nominal monthly salaries of anywhere between 50 to 100 *birr*. They work as waitresses or cashiers and sometimes do other work like washing glasses and also wait for clients on the side. They work on the basis of alternating schedules, taking turns at morning and evening shifts.

Generally one group of the women comes in the morning and works up to three or four in the afternoon and the group that takes over works through the evening up to midnight or two o'clock. The other subcategory of women, known as አሻሻጮች (sales helpers) is made up of women who come to the hotel/bar early in the evening and stay up to closing time. These women are not regarded as employees of the hotel/bar in the strict sense of the word; they are neither paid nor expected to work as waitresses. They come to the bar as a sort of sales-women and their task is to help the bar owner sell drinks to customers. However, once they have "signed on" with the hotel to work for the day this subcategory of women is expected to adhere to working hours strictly and cannot come and go as they please. As facilitators of sales, they are expected to drink and prompt the male clientele to drink.

This organization of work in the hotel/bars combines the above organization of labor with the use of the venue for the delivery of sexual services. Most hotels/bars would have rooms in their backyards that would be available for women and their clients both for short-term and overnight occupancy. The typical operational rule is that any woman who seeks to make use of a room for a short session with a client would be given a break from work. In this case the benefit that accrues to the hotel/bar is in the form of fees that the clients pay to use the rooms. However, if any of the women wants to leave the premises of the hotel/bar for any length of time, or if she wants to stay away from work for extended period of time within the premises she would be charged exit fees that range from 5-15 *birr*, the women refer to these payments as "መውጫ:መቁረጥ" ("getting exit tickets"). In most places, the fees that are paid differ on the basis of the time at which the women want to leave and on the basis of whether the departure means discontinuing work for the remainder of the day or night. Generally those who ask to leave after 10:30 or 11:00 pm will pay less than those who might want to leave early and those who return will be charged less than those who leave for good.

These conditions of work create an environment for sex work quite different from all the other types of work that I have described so far. One is that the relationship between the owner and the sex worker is not directly related to her income from sex work. It is primarily pegged on a contract that makes the labor of the women available to the owners for a specific duration of time. The payment that the women make every time they want to leave before the hour is, therefore, at least theoretically, payment for "breach of contract" on the part of the women. The owners could be said to be collecting rental fees from the women who use the hotel/bar as a venue for sex work but, unlike the pimps or the madams running the other types of sex work, do not make claims on the women's earnings from sex work *per se* or from the movements of the women after working hours. In short, the income that hotel/bar owners get from sex work is indirect, not direct.

The other difference between this category of sex work and some of the other types discussed above is that the venue gives some room for the women to operate in a relatively more secure and safe environment. A woman who waits on men in a bar or sits and entertains men for varying lengths of time would have a greater chance to assess the personalities and the dispositions of their clients than would be the case with asphalt women who had to jump into vehicles with people they have not even talked to for a while. Women who work in bars would also usually provide services within the premises of the hotel/bar, and would tend to operate in very familiar environments.

These circumstances permit the women in this category of sex work to operate with less agitation and greater composure than, say, the asphalt workers or the *akafay*. That is why the women who work in hotels/bars tend to describe themselves as " የተከበርን" (the respected) and work in hotels/bars as "የተከበረ" (dignified). The women operating out of this venue will also be able to have greater control over the terms of service to the client, including the use of condoms or other means of self-protection. Moreover, the fact that the bars/hotels tend to become regular places of work for the women creates conditions in which the women build up regular clientele or customers. These regular relationships tend to create conditions that sometimes lead to enduring unions that provide the women with exit from commercial sex.

Bar women charge for services at a rate that is lower than that of the asphalt women but a little higher than that of the *akafay* or the *bala-alga* women. For short sessions the going rate is around 50 *birr* whereas overnight service is sold for a range of 75 to 120 *birr*.

6.2 Household and Domesticity

Women who work out of small hotels/bars live either on the premises of the hotel/bar they work or elsewhere by themselves. Most hotels/bars would have a room or two that would be reserved as "የሴቶች:ቤት" (women's house) or "የሴቶች:ክፍል" (women's room). These rooms are not, generally speaking, meant to be residential quarters. They are meant to be resting places for the women or as places where women who have not found themselves clients spend the night after the midnight end of work. However, many women, who do not have any other place to go to in the morning, end up using the rooms as residence. In any case, the rooms that are made available would usually not accommodate more than a tiny fraction of the women who work in the establishment, so that women often find themselves compelled to rent a place individually or in groups somewhere close by. For those women who do stay in "the women's rooms" on a regular basis, home takes the form of a crowded hostel full of the inconveniences of life lived out of suitcases.

Women who live outside of the premises of the hotel/bar they work, be it in groups or individually, would set up household in various different ways. Some live with other members of family or relatives, others live as roommates or privately. As with all other categories of sex workers who separate their venue of work from their residence, the situation enables these women also to try to work around the stigma of commercial sex and to make a living without suffering the humiliations at both ends.

6.3 Profiles

The majority of women in this category of sex workers are born and brought up in Addis Ababa. Out of my sample of women, 71% were locally born while 29% were immigrants. They are also within the same range of youth as those who work on the asphalt or out of the big hotels and nightclubs. The average age for the group is 23 years.

The women in this category are also the most educated of the women in all the categories: some 57% had some kind of secondary education. Of these 43% had actually completed high school. 29% had elementary education. Only 14% did not have any schooling at all. Most women in this category (57%), like the others, say that they were pushed into this work for lack of alternative employment. 28.5% claimed to have followed the example of a friend. Some 14% said that they were lured into it unknowingly. Yet, as with most of the other categories, the majority of women in this category (57%) had tried some other kind of work before commercial sex and found the latter to be better paying and more permissive of freedom of action. A significant minority (43%) had not tried any other work before becoming sex workers.

The largest majority of women in this group are not only connected to but also live with family members of one kind or another. 86% said that they maintain contact with their folks and 57% said that they live with parents or siblings. Interestingly, about 43% of them said that their folks know of their work, while 67% said that it was a secret.

An interesting phenomenon about this group is that they carry the least burden in terms of full-time dependents. Only 14% said that they have persons (almost all children) who fully depend on them. However, an overwhelming majority of the women (about 86%) said that there are people who depend on them partially. For many these partial dependents were more than one person.

Overall, the sex worker that works out of the small hotels/bars of Addis Ababa today is likely to be a young woman who had some high school background. She is likely to be indigenous to Addis Ababa and commutes to work from some place where she lives with her family members.

7   Sex Work out of Drinking Places and the Women Behind it

7.1   Venues and conditions of Work

There is a very striking similarity between the category just discussed and this category in terms of all the variables. The small drinking places operate in ways that are very similar and parallel to the bars. The only difference is that most of the people who run small (usually single room) bars are women who themselves had been or are still practicing sex workers. The other point of difference with the bars is that in the small drinking places, work heats up rather late at night and might continue into the morning hours.

As in the hotels/bars, the small drinking places bring in two groups of women, one permanent, the other transient or mobile. The permanent sex workers reside in the drinking place, in a room or rooms that might be located somewhere in the back of the house. They are also provided with basic necessities like food but are not, as a rule, paid monthly salaries. However, because the permanent sex workers in the small drinking places are resident and their contact with the owners is continuous, they perform a considerable amount of domestic labor for the owners. For this reason, the arrangement appears to combine elements of (unremunerated) domestic work with those of sex work. Due to the ambiguous position of the women (as part domestics and part resident sex workers) a number of elements come into the picture that tend either to complicate the relationship between employer and worker or to make the arrangement tolerable for both. Elements that could complicate the relationship are related to the fact that the women are not paid for the domestic work and that there is no guarantee that they would be treated fairly in terms of living conditions and food. If income from the sex work is not steady or significant, these conditions might make the women feel the exploitative nature of the relationship and seek to move away from it.

However, there are also elements that could work in the other direction to make the conditions tolerable. One of these, for instance, is that the owners generally tend to recruit women whose background they know or whose behaviors they could predict. Recruitment techniques include verifying the regional or ethnic background of the woman and her previous history. Arrangements between women who come from the same part of the country tend to work out better than others because they create a shared ground on which affective ties might be built. In fact, where this shared ground exists and where a woman is believed to be attracting a lot of customers, she might expect occasional gifts or some other forms of good handling from the owner. In fact, she might be treated in such a way as to make her feel like a friend and family rather than like an outsider.

Due to limitations of space, the number of such permanent workers in small drinking places cannot be large. In fact, for most places there would not be more than one or two. Therefore, depending on the location and on felt need, the madam might allow two or three other women to come regularly or irregularly and spend time in her place, helping to facilitate sales along the way. Some of these women might also be working as asphalt women or freelancing in other venues. But some could be fairly regular, so that a situation similar to the bars, in which regular but non-employee women arrive at peak hours, develops.

A drinking place may or may not have attached rooms to be used as venue for sexual services. If such venues exist, the owner of the place benefits from room rentals. Often, however, the housing situation in Addis is such that most of these places do not have beds to rent. The women would go with the clients to other venues in the general neighborhood and would follow them to their residences only if they have developed a degree of familiarity with them.

As in the small hotels/bars, the women in small drinking places would have sufficient time to develop rapport with their clients and negotiate terms with them. Not only does this decrease their work-related insecurity, but it also makes it possible for the women to carry themselves with relatively more composure and dignity than, say, the asphalt workers or the *akafay*.

The rates at which the women who work out of this venue are remunerated vary considerably. The permanent workers charge at rates that is very similar to those of working in the bars while the transient "visitors" tend to ask payments similar to the asphalt workers.

7.2   Household and Domesticity

For the women who reside permanently in the drinking places, household arrangements take two forms, depending on whether or not the owner lives on the site. If the owner resides on the site, the amount of domestic work expected from them outside of work hours might be relatively high. However, correspondingly, the freedom of the women to entertain clients or to go out with them would increase. On the other hand, if the owner lives elsewhere, the women might be called upon to shorten the times they spend with clients or even cancel their engagements with them to attend to domestic chores or to look after the place. These matters sometimes complicate relationships and lead to their break up.

However, there is one element that appears to work towards the stability of the arrangement in many cases, and that is related to the possibility that the arrangement might accommodate the dependents of the women, particularly their children. One of my findings was that a relatively large number of women in this category (75%) have children and that their children live with them where they work.

For the women who come to the drinking places for work from external residences the arrangements of household are as varied as those for women in the other categories. Some live with parents, some with relatives and some by themselves. Some are unattached while others have intimate relationships with men that include residing together.

105

7.3 Profiles

The distinction between resident sex workers and the transient (or mobile) ones is important in the profiling of the women in this category. This is in part because the resident workers tend to be predominantly migrants to the city and the transient visitors tend to be women who are indigenous. In my sample the figures add up to almost fifty-fifty. The immigrants to the city tend to have been around for significantly long periods of time. About 50% of them said, in fact, that they had lived in Addis for over a decade. The resident immigrants are also more likely to be less educated than the "visiting" city women. 25% of the respondents in my sample did not have any schooling while another 25% dropped out of elementary schools. The remaining 50% have some education at secondary level.

There does not seem to be a major difference between the two sub-categories in terms of age, although the average age for the category as a whole (29 years) is remarkably higher than the average ages of most other categories. In fact, the category constitutes the second oldest category of sex workers in the city. Information about the causes of entry to commercial sex coming from this group is not very different from women in the other categories. 50% said they became sex workers because they were unable to find other work. Another 50% said that they followed a friend into it. Yet, like women in many of the other categories, 75% of the women in this category had tried another line of work before and 50% describe commercial sex both as better paying and as permissive of relative freedom.

A striking 100% of the women in this category maintain contact with family and kin. Equally strikingly, all the 100% of them said that their family members and close relatives either openly knew that they were sex workers or knew the facts even if they did not acknowledge them openly. A similar situation about dependents applies here also. All the 100% of the respondents in my sample said that they support other people either entirely or partially.

In general, the women who sell sex out of the hundreds of small drinking places that line up the avenues and back streets of Addis Ababa are likely to be two types: type one is likely to be a young woman in her late twenties or early thirties who had arrived from rural Ethiopia some time ago; she is likely to be unschooled and burdened with responsibility for a child. She is likely to be living where she works and functions in an ambiguous position as part-domestic part-sex worker. Type two is likely to be a young woman of about the same age who lives in the neighborhoods with parents or relatives and who comes out in the evenings to do "business". She is highly likely to be a high-school drop out who feels compelled to go out and earn some money either to support her impoverished parents or to keep her siblings in school or, quite commonly, to feed her own child born out of wedlock.

8 Conclusion

In this chapter I have tried to bring out the different forms and facets of sex work in Addis Ababa to the extent that my numerical and qualitative data (and space) have permitted. The data that I presented show that the face of commercial sex in Addis Ababa has changed considerably since scholars like Laketch Diresse and Andargatchew Tesfaye studied it some thirty years ago. The most remarkable change that has occurred since then is not in the external form of sex work or, as conventionally referred to, in the "types". For, the various "types" that I have listed above are not so radically different from the lists that were composed by Laketch or Andargatchew. The most remarkable change is in the content of each of the types or in the way sex work is organized internally. These substantive changes came about due mainly to the expansion of urban poverty over the last quarter century or more and the further complications created by the housing regime that has been in place in the city. Urban poverty meant that more and more of the city's sex workers are indigenous to the city. Whereas in the past Addis Ababa's sex workers were made up mainly of unschooled immigrants, now they are predominantly made up of city-born school dropouts. Whereas in the past the reasons for women's entry into commercial sex were to be sought mainly in rural socio-economic conditions, now they have to be sought mainly in urban socio-economic conditions. The problem of housing, on the other hand, complicates the ways in which the women who are drawn into commercial sex fit themselves into it; that is because lack of control over venues narrows the options available to the women and forces them either to be immobile or to negotiate terms of operation with those that control the venues.

One of the implications of these changes, which keep showing itself in each of the types that I have described above, is the differentiation of the sex business into two broad varieties in terms of the operational style of the women and their remuneration. One variety, dominated by women who grew up in the city itself, appears to be mobile, dexterous, and very adaptable to different venues of work. It takes the women from the residential neighborhoods to the streets, to the big hotels, to the nightclubs as well as to the small bars and roadside drinking houses. It also takes them back and forth between different venues, sometimes within a single night. Because the women who engage in it are mostly city-born, they seek to make the most of what the city's leisure and entertainment industry has to offer. They tend to be, therefore, less conservatively anchored to specific venues and more floating and diffuse. They also tend to be better paid for the services they render.

The other variety of sex work, dominated mainly by uneducated (or very poorly educated) women with rural background, tends to be less mobile, anchored to specific locations and therefore conservative. It operates from neighborhoods into which procurers bring young girls who are not familiar with the city's social and geographical terrain. The women who practice it tend to be immobile and subject to drudgery. They tend to be poor, demoralized and very poorly remunerated for the services they give.

The other implication of the changes since the 1970s', also showing itself in the above discussion of the various types of sex work, is the expansion of control over the incomes of the sex workers and over their freedom of movement by other "stakeholders". In the two most common forms of sex work, namely *akafay* and asphalt work, the sex business is actually run and controlled by sexual entrepreneurs (the madams and the pimps) who assert direct control over the incomes that the women get from selling sex. *One of them exploits its control over indoor space (i.e. control over housing); the other exploits its control over outdoor space (i.e. exploits the dangerousness of the streets).* The fact that the women often use the language of affection when talking about these people is beside the point. In the other types of sex work too, the women have to negotiate access to venues either by paying or by working for those who control them; thus they are charged for moving between and among venues in small hotels, bars and nightclubs, or exploited in the form of unpaid domestic work in the small drinking places. It is also clear from the details provided in this chapter that woman in all the various types of sex work are exposed to greater and greater exploitation by those who have direct or indirect control over residential space.

All of these conditions also have very important and serious implications for the way sex workers negotiate the social space, a negotiation made even more complex by the fact that sex work is associated with stigma and shame. I will address these issues in the following chapter.

Chapter Five

Negotiating Social Space: Sex Workers and the Social Context of Sex Work in Addis Ababa

There are three principal points on which there is almost complete unanimity among the sex workers of Addis Ababa today. One of these is that sex work is a kind of work that a woman undertakes for compelling economic reasons irrespective of how she actually comes into it; it is not an occupation on which one embarks as a matter of pure choice. The other is that sex work is shameful; it is degrading to the woman herself as well as to all those she is related to. The third is that sex work is not a lifetime career; it is a temporary undertaking that one should get out of as quickly as possible.

In this chapter I will describe the ways in which the women with whom I have worked interpret and interact with different sections of society on the basis of these three principles. I will argue that the social personality of individual sex workers is determined by the way they try to reconcile these widely-shared principles with the reality in which they find themselves today. I will show that this effort to reconcile the principles with reality produces three different approaches by the women in their dealings with society. One of the approaches, which I will call *affirmative*, is one in which the women try to maintain and/or reinforce their relationship with certain categories of people despite the disruptive nature of sex work. The second approach, to which I will refer as *isolationist*, is one in which the women are compelled to avoid contact or interaction with a certain category of people and therefore limit their social relationships with them. The third approach, which I will call *interactive*, is one in which the women engage in active social relationships with a variety of people with whom they come into contact as part of their daily life. The three approaches are not items in a list out of which the women can choose. All of them are pursued concurrently, or at the same time. What this means is that for each woman who engages in commercial sex, life is partly about maintaining some types of previously existing social relationship (thus, affirmative); partly it is about temporarily moving away from some types of social relationship (thus, isolationist); and partly about creating or actively pursuing some types of social relationship (thus interactive).

110

I have set myself two tasks in this chapter. First, I will identify the types of social relationship that the women tend to affirm, to avoid, or to pursue. As I do so, I will draw on the life-stories that I collected to present the arguments that the women put forward in justification of their decisions in each case. Second, I will describe the strategies that the women employ in pursuit of their objectives and what costs and benefits these strategies entail for them. I will pursue these tasks at two levels. At the first level I will talk about individual women. At the second level, I will talk about categories of women. On both levels of discussion, I will try to show the relevance of the variables that I have used in chapter 3 for the differentiation of the women and the categories that have resulted from the use of those variables as described in chapter 4. The materials at both levels complement each other and reinforce the idea of differentiating sex workers as well as their social behaviors.

1 Affirming Social Ties: The Dilemmas and Strategies of Sustained Contact

Listening to sex workers as they tell the story of why and how they started work and why they are still working, one cannot fail to notice a deeply moral element. That moral element is the commitment of the women to the well being of their immediate kin, particularly to members of their families. For many women, the basic reason both for entering commercial sex and for staying in it is to provide for loved ones who stand in critical need of material support. The material conditions of many households have gotten so desperate, and poverty so deeply entrenched, that teenage girls find themselves compelled to do something about it, even if this means taking up commercial sex work and thus confronting another moral dilemma. In some cases the sex worker would be a daughter who is trying to give a helping hand to a family that is struggling to survive in deep economic adversity; in some others she would be a sister who is trying to feed and clothe siblings who have been left helpless by the death of one or both of their parents; still in others, it could be a mother who is determined to take care of her child or children.

Alemtsehay is a 23 year-old young woman who was born and brought up in Addis Ababa in the house of her parents. She operates out of a hotel in downtown Addis not far from the neighborhood in which she had grown up. This is how she explains for her entry into sex work.

I have been in this work now for the last three years. Before that, I had worked as a maid for two years. I quit school when I was in the 11th grade because my father died and our family of three children was stranded financially. Before his death my father worked for *Kiray Betoch* [i.e. the office that administers government rental houses] as a carpenter. He was poorly paid, but at least there was something to eat. My mother also helped by selling *tella*. After the death of my father, mother's lone struggle to keep three children fed and clothed became an impossible fight. Her health also deteriorated. I simply could not continue in school while all of us were starving. I decided to find work and keep my sister and brother in school. Since then I have been the main source of income for the family. All members of my family know that I am in this business.

Almaz is a sex worker who lives in the famous sex worker neighborhood of *Katanga*. She works in a small kiosk where she also lives with her 13 year-old daughter. She tells a similar story of being driven into sex work by parental poverty.

I was born in Jimma to a very poor family. My father had no work at all. Only occasionally did he work as a farm-hand for rich people. My mother worked as a domestic and sometimes sold *tella*. We were miserable. I was the oldest child in the house. I had two siblings. There were times that we did not have anything at all to eat. I came to Addis Ababa with my godmother who promised to send me to school. However, things did not work out. Nor could I forget the misery in which my parents and siblings lived. So I took up employment as a domestic for a monthly salary of 10 *birr*. Since I ate and lived where I worked it was possible for me to save all the money and send it off to my folks every two or three months. Alas, after a while I could not bear the pain and suffering in the house of my employers. I went off to a *dalala* house looking for another job. I ended up in this area where I started work as an *akafay*. Unfortunately I got pregnant soon after. The father of my daughter went off to the war front and never returned. I ended up having to take care of myself and my daughter. As a result I had to interrupt the support to my parents. It has been 13 years now since I lost contact with them. I don't know if they are dead or alive. Currently I am completely devoted to my daughter. She is the only family I have. I am working to provide for her and to keep her in school.

Yeshi is a migrant to Addis Ababa. She has been in sex work for the last four years. She is illiterate but very highly committed to her family back in Raya, Wollo.

I come from Raya Almata. I came into this kind of life owing to the poverty of my family. My parents had 10 children of whom 3 had died and 7 survived. When I first came here I took up employment as a domestic for 20 *birr* a month around the French Legation. I was not able to stay in it for more than two months. Then I became a baby-sitter for a salary of 30 *birr* a month. Then I shifted to another household for a slightly better salary of 35 *birr*. All of this money I dutifully sent to my folks. Every time someone came to Addis from my home region I would seek them out and send money to my folks. For quite sometime I was not able to buy myself so much as a pair of slippers. I shifted from place to place in domestic work and reached a salary of 75 *birr* working as a cleaner in a restaurant. Still I was never able to improve my lot because I was sending money to my folks. Eventually it was a woman who worked with me in the restaurant who encouraged me to go to the *dalala* house to look for a better job. ... I ended up in *Doro Manaqia* with an old woman for whom I worked as an *akafay*. I took up the work because I thought I might be able to support my folks relatively easily. I tell you, I came into this work for the sake of my folks. I am still in it for them. I have tried a number of times to get them out of poverty. Still my dream is to see them live better. I am prepared to accept a sacrifice even greater than HIV, a sacrifice that might even result in my immediate death, as long as I can help bring better days for my folks

113

Fantu H is 22. She is the oldest of five children orphaned by the death of both their parents. She was born and brought up in the slum neighborhood of *Cherqos*, in Addis Ababa. This is how she explains her entry into asphalt work:

> I came out into the asphalt about 7 years ago because both of our parents died and I was the oldest child. I have two brothers and two sisters. I have to do something to support them. The two boys do shoe-shinning after school; but the two girls can't do anything. For sometime, I tried to vend *jebillo* (i.e. cigarettes, soft paper, gums, etc), but it was not enough to feed us and keep my brothers and sisters in school.

In all the four examples above, the motive is to preserve or maintain family, something that is deeply valued by society as a whole. In all the above cases, the women interpret what they are doing as acts of sacrifice (not of adventure), acts of sacrifice that are expected of a daughter, a sister or a mother. From their respective points of view, what they were doing to save their parents, their siblings or their children from starvation, humiliation or possible death is deeply moral; it is something that they would be proud of rather than ashamed of. By the same token, the most painful condition to be in for a woman who does this kind of work is to fail to provide even minimal support for people to whom she owes it. I will pick up this theme in the following section.

The morality behind the actions of the women in the above four cases (as well as in many others) comes out even more strongly when one considers the fact that there is no material benefit of any kind or any other kind of reward that comes to the women from what they do. In other words, this is not an act of transaction in which someone does something in the hope of getting something in return. In fact, it is an act in which a sacrifice of the most serious kind is consciously accepted for the redemption of others. Yeshi's remark that she is prepared to accept a sacrifice "even greater than HIV, a sacrifice that might even result in my immediate death as long as I can help bring better days for my folks" is both pertinent and powerful in this context.

It is one thing to sacrifice oneself for the sake of one's loved ones and to resolve the moral dilemmas thereof individually; it is quite another matter, however, to expect that those for whom the sacrifice is made

114

would appreciate it and accept the social costs (for them) of the action. Several women to whom I have talked have faced this serious dilemma. The strategy that most of them have adopted to deal with the dilemma is hiding information from the beneficiaries themselves about what they do to earn an income, or, alternatively, telling them that they were doing something else. Two of the women whom I have referred to above, as well as several others who tell similar stories, have adopted this strategy. Yeshi told both her father and mother, who came to visit at different times, that she works in a pastry shop. Almaz, who does sex work in a tiny house in which she lives with her daughter, struggles to have her daughter believe that she makes a living by washing clothes for other people and by vending potatoes and onions; she keeps telling her that the men who sleep in their house at night are renting beds for the night.

In many cases, this misrepresentation might help and the burden can be considerably reduced if there is some physical distance between the woman and her folks. It is thus easier for immigrant women (like Yeshi, above) rather than for those who are indigenous to the city or for those who live with family members in the same house (like Almaz). However, sometimes these misrepresentations do not work well, and many difficult and embarrassing moments occur. This is what Yeshi says about how she suffered during her mother's visit to Addis.

> It was very difficult. I had to devise a strategy to have my mother spend the night somewhere else rather than in my house. It was impossible for me to close shop and sit with my mother for the duration of her visit. That would mean no income for the whole time and also nothing to give to my mother when she leaves. What I did was tell my mother that I worked night shift at the pastry shop and that there is a roommate of mine who comes and sleeps on the single bed in the house at night. I begged a woman who is my neighbor to let my mother pass the nights in her house. The woman was generous, and allowed me to do so...My mother, however, did not want to go, insisting that she can sleep with my roommate on the bed. I had to discourage her, telling her that my roommate disliked sharing a bed with anyone. Finally, my mother did go to my neighbor's house. Unfortunately, my mother discovers that this neighbor of mine is a Muslim and found it impossible to stay in the house.

The woman also wore heavy perfume, to which my mother had some kind of allergic reaction. Imagine the embarrassment of my mother leaving the house of my neighbor and coming to my house late at night while I was sleeping with a client. That is exactly what happened. Fortunately, some neighborhood kids alerted me about my mother's coming. I had barely enough time to chase the man out of the house and have a young girl next door come and lie down on my bed so that my mother would think of the girl as my roommate. Finally we pretended as if my "roommate" was leaving the bed for my mother. For the remainder of the time that my mother was in town, I had to find another place and work as *akafay*. She slept on my bed. I was really very hurt and angry that my own parents, for whom I was going through all of this, did not appreciate my condition and make things even harder for me. I cried a lot alone about this.

Almaz , who has an even harder time trying to live with a 13 year-old young girl in very small quarters in which she combines sex work with bed-renting, talks at length about the difficulties, the risks and the embarrassments of such a life.

My nights are sleepless nights. I try to keep what is going on from my daughter. I go out and stand at the door after I have put her to sleep. Sometimes fights break out with the men and my daughter is woken up. I try to tell her that the fights happen because somebody was refusing to pay for the bed. But the men shout out the word *shermuta*, and declare loudly that the fights were about payment for sex. There are also times when someone rents the bed and sleeps in the house before I have found a client for the night. When this happens I have no choice but to give up going out to solicit because I fear for the safety of my daughter. There was this time when I took a risk and went out briefly. When I returned, I found a man trying to rape my daughter. From that time on I stopped going out to solicit if there is a man in the house. You see, I cannot allow my fate to be the fate of my daughter also.

Under these kinds of conditions it is difficult to believe that the people whose feelings the women are trying to protect through these acts of misrepresentation do not know or sense what is going on. It will not be wide off the mark to assume that a "conspiracy of silence" surrounds the situation, a conspiracy in which the woman does not tell and the beneficiaries do not ask. In short, a situation develops in which both parties understand each other without talking. This is what partly explains why a very significant number of women said that their folks knew what they did, but did not acknowledge it openly or "officially".

The other strategy, equally common, is to let the beneficiaries know what the woman actually does to put some food on the table. A strikingly significant number of women said that they practiced commercial sex with the open knowledge of their family and kin. In this scenario, the two parties might join together in keeping "the secret" from others. This might include making arrangements about housing and venues of work that would save the family some of the embarrassments. Fantu H, the woman who took up sex work to keep her sisters and brothers in school, has chosen this strategy.

> I do not live with my brothers and sisters. I live with four other women who do asphalt work like me. I do this partly for the well-being of my siblings. You know it is not good for them if I came home in bad shape, drunk or drugged. I try to protect them from pain. It is also not good for our image in the neighborhood. As it is our neighbors talk a lot about me doing this at such a young age. Coming home at 4 or 5 in the morning is not going to help that already bad image.

Many times, however, such arrangements might not be possible, either for lack of housing or for lack of sufficient resources, leading to an open engagement in sex work out of residences shared with one's family. Indeed, in many cases, the work might be done inside the residence itself, not just out of it. It is not uncommon for the woman to be both the household head as well as the only bread-earner. When this happens, sex work is combined with domestic responsibilities at home, including the nursing of the old or of the young.

Despite the differences that these various mechanisms of synchronizing sex work with domestic conditions create among the

117

women, there is considerable evidence that the women who seek to maintain old ties through such acts of sacrifice share similarities in terms of their family background and the causes and circumstances of their entry into commercial sex. Many, like Yeshi, Almaz, and Fantu H, grew up in stable families where there was good care and love; they did not have a background of broken families or of growing up in families where there was disharmony and conflict. Women like this would also explain their entry into commercial sex either in terms of economic difficulties encountered by the family as a whole or in terms of crises created by the death of one or both of the parents. Almaz entered the sex business due to the impoverishment of her parents. For Fantu H, the story is different. She ended up with sex work because her parents died one after another and she found herself in charge of five people with nothing at hand.

In the great majority of cases, however, the social ties for which these kinds of sacrifices are made are ties with one's offspring. There is more than sufficient evidence that sex workers take care of their children and that many, in fact, take up sex work specifically for that purpose. Needless to say, sex workers could have children both before and after entry in to the work. For that reason, it is not possible to determine whether commercial sex follows or precedes parentage.   Prior to the recent widespread use of condoms for health reasons, the greatest source of insecurity for sex workers, particularly for those with little or no knowledge of birth control, was pregnancy. As it often happens, a child born in the course of sex work is unlikely to have its paternity known or acknowledged. In my sample of 23 women who had children after they became sex workers, 8 (34.7%) reported that they did not know the fathers of their children while 14 (60.8%) said that they knew the fathers but that the latter would not recognize paternity.

As has happened with many of my informants, children could also be produced during short periods of withdrawal from sex work either due to marriage or due to an extended period of intimacy with individual men. One of the key factors for return to sex work after abandoning it for long or short periods of time is lack of support for child-rearing expenses. However, a good many women are also mothers prior to their engagement in commercial sex. In any case, the raising of children would always entail economic burdens on the women irrespective of where the children stay, while in many cases it forces the women to re-link with family and kin, with former husband/boyfriends or even former in-laws for one or another kind of support. In fact, the sheer difficulty of raising children while practicing commercial sex makes children the nodal point of reconnection between the women and a variety of other people.

Although the key relationship of dependence into which sex workers get is the one between them and their children, it should be stated, however, that we see women who practice commercial sex also striving to maintain or reinforce social ties with parents, siblings, relatives and friends. We see also that proceeds from sex work go in varying proportions to finance the maintenance or reinforcement of these ties. Of these ties, the one that sounds least compelling is the one among friends. However, there are very striking stories of personal sacrifice by sex workers to advance a friend or of standing by her side at times of severe adversity. Tigist, one of my informants, states that her friend was, in her mind, much more than a sister to her:

> I loved my friend so much that you can say that I lived for her. I was regularly in her house and rarely stayed away from her for more than a few hours. There are a number of times that I bought clothing, shoes or other materials for her even though I stood in need of them myself. I even went further and supported her family with the money that I made by selling my body. All of this was out of loyalty to our long-standing friendship.

It is tempting to say that this or that category of sex workers is more or less likely to engage in social ties on a sustained basis. However, from the evidence that I have, it is difficult to make any firm statements about this. Of course, the figures quoted in chapter 4 show that a greater number of women who are native to Addis Ababa (those who tend to predominate in asphalt, hotel and nightclub sex work and constitute the mobile element in the other categories also) tend to live with their parental families than those in the other categories (like the various types of *akafay* and independent operators). But living with parental families does not *necessarily* indicate that social ties are financed by sex work or that these ties are necessarily strong. All we can say on the basis of these figures is that city-born women who function in the mobile and transient types of sex work have a greater degree of interaction with their family members or other close kin. We can also say that their social ties have a higher chance of escaping disruption to a greater extent than those of the settled or conservative groups because many could function without referring to themselves as fully-fledged sex workers.

2 Putting Social Ties On Hold: The Dilemmas and Strategies of Avoidance

Sex work, as I stated at the beginning of this chapter, is universally regarded as a shameful and demeaning work. Every one of the women that I talked to in the in-depth interviews affirmed this. There was not a single woman who intimated to me that she went into the business because she wanted to be in it or because she enjoyed it. All the women that I interviewed were unanimous on this point; so much so that I find it very disturbing that some authors have made statements about "prostitution" being culturally "tolerated" in Ethiopia or about some prostitutes being nymphomaniacs.

Every one of the women that I interviewed also said that she has suffered, or is still suffering, from the stigma associated with sex work. For them, the most important point of complaint is that society looks only at *the fact* of their involvement in sex work without taking into consideration the compelling reasons that drive them into it.

There are always people in the lives of sex workers whom the latter associate with this public bias against sex work and thus avoid dealing with. In many cases, these are close relatives of the women, people who are related to them by blood. However, they could also be non-relatives who might have grown up with them or known them in childhood. Sex workers choose the strategy of avoidance with these categories of people in part because there are no compelling reasons for sustaining direct or regular contact; it is, therefore, possible to keep the relationship at a distance. In part, however, it is because a wide circle of relatives or old acquaintances is simply too unmanageable or too broad to convince or to share secrets with.

Ironically, however, the circle might sometimes include the family members of the women, at times even including the very people who depend partly or fully on the incomes of the women. When this happens, the frustration on the part of the women is high because avoiding these people is not altogether possible, and difficult moments, of the kind that I described above, might occur. But there are women who do, indeed, avoid all of their folks, family as well as kin, friends as well as acquaintances, and thus withdraw totally from the social circle within which they had lived prior to taking up commercial sex.

The explanations for these withdrawals are varied. For some like Fantu G it is because these are rustic or rural people (ባላገሮች) who are not knowledgeable about urban conditions and therefore cannot be told what is going on. For others, like Marta, these are parents or relatives who are hard and rigid (የማይገባቸው) and thus who cannot understand the reasoning of the women for being in this line of work.

An interesting dimension of avoidance as a social condition is its relationship with the economic status or material condition of the women. Many of the women say that avoiding their kin and relatives becomes their only option in part because they have little to show for their engagement in this difficult and degrading work. In other words, not only are they living in shame but are also very poor. They say that it would have been easier to negotiate a degree of acceptability with one's kin if sex work had been materially rewarding or if the women could achieve a degree of material prosperity that can be shown off or shared with others. The poorer the women become, the further the gap between them and their relatives.

Sometimes contacts are lost and communication broken not because of entry into sex work per se but because the woman has become increasingly unable to make ends meet and therefore totally unable to respond to the consequences of maintaining the contact. Here is what Fantu G, a sex worker who has been in the trade for over twenty years and who declares that she has relatives "all over the place", had to say about why her relationship with them has nevertheless virtually come to a freeze:

> I can't say I have kin here except *Medhanealem* [i.e. Savior of the World, or Christ]. I am telling you, I don't have any one except Him. My folks, well, I don't want to see them. You know why? It is because I don't have anything at hand. I have neither a house nor other property with which I can entertain my guests. I have nothing to eat myself; I live on what chance brings my way. What will I do if my relatives come to me and say this or that sad thing has happened to so and so, that I should go visit him? What will I do if they come and say to me that there is a happy occasion in the house of so and so? What will I

take along by way of congratulations? I have nothing whatsoever. What will I give them by way of transportation fare if they come here visiting me? Nothing. So, my friend that is why I hide my whereabouts from everybody. If I had something at hand, nobody could have competed with me for the number of relatives.

The story of Almaz, the woman who now says that she has "nobody to call a relative", is not much different from that of Fantu. However, it does illustrate an extreme case of isolation borne of inability to maintain contact for purely material reasons. When she first came from Jimma, says Almaz,

> I was so determined to help my parents. As I said to you, I sent every *santim* that I made to them. Then I got pregnant and became a mother myself. It is hard enough to raise a child in my situation. There is nobody to support or help me. I have no idea whether my parents are alive or dead. I am completely cut off. My daughter keeps asking me about them. She says how come only the two of us exist without any relatives. She worries what will happen to her if I died. She keeps begging me to take her to Jimma to meet my folks. But I can't afford to do that. I can't even afford the transport money.

Unlike Almaz, for most women the isolation from one's folks is not believed to be final. Relationships are put on hold because of the current inconvenience only. They are renewable when and if conditions permit. These conditions could take the form of material well-being within sex work or of exiting sex work and engaging in gainful employment of some kind. The timetable is often left to God, the most frequent expression being "እሱ:ያለ:ለታ" (When He so wills). I was, however, always struck by the confidence with which the women expressed their chances of reconnecting with their folks as soon as they either left sex work or got prosperous within it. Fantu G who says that she left home እንደዋዛ (casually) says that all it takes for her to have her folks streaming to Addis Ababa to see her is "addressing a letter to my father and having it dropped by the bus station in the town; he is so well-known that any police officer by the bus station would hand it over to him; I hope, one day, that will happen". Yeshi S tells a story about how she bravely joined a *mahber* (association) of her kin in Addis Ababa and how she managed to keep a good relationship with them without actually showing them her residence or telling them what she did to make a living. "When it was my turn to host the members of the *mahber*", she says, "I called upon the help of a friend who has a decent house somewhere in the city".

What is interesting is that even those women whose entry into sex work has been discovered by their family, kin and relatives and have thus been forced into isolation, expressed confidence that they could easily make up with them and rejoin their folks if it becomes necessary. Many of them said that they will simply ask for forgiveness and get back, the frequent expression being: "ምን፡ችግር፡አለ? ታርቄ፡እገባለሁ" (There is no problem at all; I can make peace with them easily!). Selamawit, who had left home because she was tired of her mother's nagging, returned to her mother several times, only to leave home again and return to sex work. Her latest return was caused by her pregnancy.

Families or relatives who are avoided by sex workers are also kept in mind by the latter as a fall-back option, that is, as a social world they would rejoin if things get worse and life becomes impossible. I was told several times by the women that their friends who had recently died had gone off to their relatives when their conditions got hopeless; there, having made up with their folks, they had died in peace.

It is this firm belief in the temporary nature of separation from one's family, relatives or friends that explains the strategies the women use to hide their identity. The most frequently used strategy is the changing of names. Many women expressed to me their belief that women in sex work rarely tell their real names to people. In fact, out of my sample of 100 women, 34 told me openly that they assume different identity at work and the most frequent way of changing identity is changing a name. 19 of these women (56%) said that the reason for this is to hide what they did from family and kin. It is also for this reason, it appears to me, that many of the women that I interviewed did not insist that I hide their names when and if I tell their stories in my work. The other equally common strategy of identity alteration is the separation of venue of work from residence and the frequent shifting of both venues.

The temporary suspension of social ties and other forms of social relationship is so widespread that it is difficult to associate certain categories of sex workers with the practice and exclude others from it. It is, however, reasonable to conclude that migrant women who tend to work in fixed locations (mostly as *akafay* and as independent operators), tend to have an easier time putting themselves in a state of social isolation than women who were born and brought up in Addis Ababa. Of course, for the latter, the size of the city also offers some protection, but is not enough to remove the risk of one day running into somebody they knew from their neighborhood.

3   Building Social Ties and Networks: The Dilemmas and Strategies of Socialization

To be in a social limbo in relation to certain categories of people does not, of course, mean that the sex worker in Addis Ababa is a lone figure with little or no engagement with society. In fact, sex work happens to be one of the most socially demanding of occupations. It is socially demanding not just because it involves physical "intimacy" with the men to whom sexual service is provided but also because it is a life of insecurity for which social support systems of all kinds is necessary. Equally importantly, the only option that sex workers have to get out of this work is to be socially active and engaged. No woman who seeks to leave this kind of life behind can afford narrowing down her social networks. To do so, in fact, will constitute closing the door of advancement on herself.

In this section, I will first provide some detail on these and other considerations behind the active social engagement of Addis Ababa's sex workers both at work and after work, and outline the value systems that guide their actions. Then, I will address the strategies that they employ to build and sustain social networks. Finally, I will show what kinds of social networks tend to be built by the various categories of sex workers and the strategies that tend to predominate in each case.

As I have pointed out several times above, for many of my informants sex work is a tough work, a kind of work involving insecurities and risks of all kind; however, it is also work that brings the women into contact with a wide range of people on a daily basis. There are four categories of people that are particularly noteworthy for this daily contact with sex workers: the men who come to them as clients, other sex workers who work and/or live with them, and neighbors who live in proximity to them. The men to whom service is given bring to the women both risks and opportunities. Women who work together can also be competitive or cooperative with each other. Sex workers can be accepted and embraced by their neighbors or marginalized and ostracized by them. The positive or negative elements in each case can be insignificant or very serious, depending on the type and condition of sex work that the women engage in, on the place and conditions of their residence, and on their individual social skills.

Men who come as clients present sex workers with a daily combination of risks and opportunities. Men could be mean, brutish and very abusing. Every woman to whom I talked has more than one story of abuse that she suffered in the hands of men. From the mean-spirited exploiters who refuse to make payments after their sexual desires have been gratified to the sexual predators who subject the women to physical agony and psychological terror, from the Casanova types who turn into parasites by domesticating themselves with the women, to pilferers and thieves who come to rob them, men come in various forms and represent varying degrees of adversity to the women. However, men who come to purchase sexual services could also be generous, kind, civil and caring individuals. Every woman that I talked to also has more than one story of generosity, kindness, civility and care involving men who had come to them as clients. From those who pay generously to those who provide psychological counsel, from those who encourage them to seek alternative employment to those who actually set them up in another field of economic activity, men come in different forms and represent different degrees of opportunity to sex workers. One of the points on which my sample of 100 women was almost unanimous (99%) was that men who come as clients vary immensely among themselves, so that it would be difficult to generalize about them.

The existence of both of these categories of men elicits different kinds of reactions from the women, reactions that manifest themselves in the ways they socialize with other people, including the men themselves. In anticipation of the men who might abuse or mistreat them, the women build relationships of friendship with people who they hope will protect them or come to their help when in need. These may be hotel guards, police officers, fellow sex workers next door or youth in the neighborhood: one of the common forms of reference to these kinds of people is "በሞህ:የሚደርሱልኝ" (those who come to my rescue when I scream for help). The insecurities of having to deal with new faces and new characters on a daily basis thus generate among sex workers compulsive socialization to ensure security. In some categories of sex work (like, for instance, asphalt work) these insecurities are particularly intense, making the building of defensive relationships almost a formal requirement. In other categories of sex work (particularly those that combine venues of work and residence) these insecurities tend to be less intense and do not need formal arrangements for protection.

Another type of social interaction generated by insecurities that are expected to come from "bad" men is interaction among the women themselves. This takes the form of exchange of information about "the bad guys". I was told by the women whom I interviewed that they routinely tell each other about the happenings of each night that they passed with men; that they make it a point, particularly, to inform other women about abusive men. 96% of the women in my sample said that they do so. "A man who has mistreated you tonight is not likely to come back to you again", says Zerfe, "he is likely to come to another woman who does not know him; it is therefore important to forewarn each other about these kinds of people." It is interesting that this circulation of information is not limited to circles of friendship or intimacy among the women. "I will warn as many women in the bar against bad men so that they don't go through the agonies that I have gone through", says Alemtsehay, a sex worker who operates from a bar. "A woman does not have to be my friend to be told about an abuser; if I keep this kind of information to myself or share it only with one or two friends, then tomorrow it will be my turn to be caught unaware".

Men who show positive dispositions towards sex workers are treated by the latter equally positively. This positive reaction to "good" men takes various forms and passes through several stages, depending on the length of time for which the relationship is sustained. A caring man who treats a woman gently and visits her fairly regularly would become a dNb¾ (*denbegna*: customer). His chances of qualifying as such will be higher if he is not involved with other women known to the particular woman he visits, and if he pays generously. A relationship with a *denbegna* does not necessarily imply emotional attachment with him; nor is the relationship with a *denbegna* necessarily known to other people or recognized by them as exclusive: other women, for instance, could go out with the man if and when he makes an overture toward them, although this rarely happens among women who are personal friends or are close to each other.

When a relationship between a woman and her *denbegna* matures further the man becomes her ወዳጅ (*wedaj*: intimate person). This stage involves both emotional attachment and wider public knowledge of the relationship. It also becomes exclusive in relation to other women, so that it is regarded as an affront or personal attack to the woman if another woman sleeps with the man. It is not, however, necessarily exclusive of other men, so that the woman would continue to sleep with other men in his absence. In some cases, however, a *wedajinet* might involve an arrangement in which the woman substantially reduces her involvement with other men or temporarily withdraws from sex work altogether for varying lengths of time. I was told that this is a fairly common phenomenon these days, particularly with women who have built long-term relationships with foreigners who come and go from Addis Ababa. The women will withdraw from active sex work during the presence of their customers and return to the active mode on their departure. In any case, what is distinctive about *wedaj* is that the man would not be overlooked in favor of other men even if these other men offered more money or made attractive promises to the woman.

When a relationship between a sex worker and her *wedaj* matures further, the latter might graduate into ፍቅረኛ (*fiqregna*: lover). A *fiqregna* is a person who is recognized as a person emotionally attached to the woman to the point of being no longer regarded as relating to her commercially. His access to the woman would be exclusive of both men and women to the extent that his presence would always make the woman totally unavailable for other men. A relationship with a *fiqregna* might also involve a flow of resources from the woman to the man and vice-versa, apparently without any accounting. It might also involve an arrangement in which the *fiqregna* resides with the woman and runs a household with her. In fact, the term ባል (*bal*: husband) is sometimes interchangeably used with *fiqregna*, indicating the regularity of the relationship and the degree of intimacy involved. Typically, a story of *fiqregninat* among sex workers will have several tortuous chapters, characterized by fights due to jealousy or failing to carry the burden of household on the part of the men. They would therefore typically end in breakup. However, some relationships do eventually graduate into successful ጋብቻ (*gabicha*: marriage) and, thus, to a final exit of the women from sex work.

From my interviews with many women, I have learnt that the majority of them (87% in my sample) were, or still are, involved in a *denbegna* relationship with several men; many also said that they had, or still have, men whom they would describe as *wedaj*. Interestingly, a very significant percentage of women also said that they had been in a *fiqregna* relationship with men at one point in their lives. In my sample, these women accounted for 41% of respondents. 12% of the women in my entire sample said that their relationship with a *fiqregna* led to the establishment of a household with them. In the case of 7% of the respondents, the household was run while the woman continued in commercial sex, while 5% reported that they withdrew from it.

It is interesting to note that the risks as well as the opportunities that are involved in the relationship of sex workers with men differ among the various categories of sex work. It so happens that the types of sex work that involve the highest risks (asphalt, hotel and nightclub work) are also the ones that provide the best opportunities. From the stories I collected in the interviews, I gathered that the best payments for sexual services as well as the fastest and the most reassuring exits from sex work were made by women who had met foreigners (referred to by the women as zɒU (*zega*: [foreign] citizen) in night clubs or in the streets. Some of these stories have happy endings in which the "liberated" women themselves try to help others liberate themselves. In the relatively less risky undertakings like *akafay*, *be-alga* or *buna-bet* sex work, etc. the progression from a *denbegna* relationship to *gabicha* tends to be slow, long and often unsuccessful.

Another category of people with whom each sex worker has to live by balancing two potentially contradictory elements of competition and cooperation is other sex workers. Sex work is a competitive business in which there are no guarantees that a woman who is successful today would be successful tomorrow also. Owing to the continuously declining market caused by the HIV phenomenon, the competition among the women tends to be tough and merciless. In my sample of 100 women, 87% said that there is vicious competition among the women and a significant 60% said that women routinely steal each other's customers. In fact, 65% said that taking each other's customers is not regarded as theft or as anything negative.

The above statistics about competition are significant. But even more significant are the statistics about solidarity or mutual support among the women. A relatively high percentage of them said that disagreements among them are minor and short. An even higher percentage (95%) said that they respect the principle of protecting each other against danger. As cited above, 96% said that they regularly inform each other about dangerous or "bad" men. An equally revealing figure of 93% of respondents said that they share what they get with women who did not get clients. What these statistics attest, without any doubt, is that, paradoxically, both competition and cooperation are getting intense as incomes from the sex market decline and as the business gets more and more dangerous.

The relationships of mutual cooperation generated by sex work take various forms and manifest themselves with various levels of intensity among the different types of sex work. Mutual support networks of economic nature focus on the sharing of clothes, shoes, cosmetics, food, beverages and stimulants. The circulation of these resources sometimes leads to the formation of friendships or small groups among women who work together. They might also lead to the organization of shared households in which the women take up residence together. The relationships are sometimes institutionalized in the form of *mahber* (association) and *iqub* (credit unions). The *mahber* could be a coffee *mahber* in which the women take turns to make coffee and invite members, or a *tsiwa mahber* in which they take turns to prepare modest feasts in honor of a saint and invite the women to it.

But the most common form is unstructured sharing of resources in which the woman who has made some money or has purchased some distributable material becomes the dispenser and the others become receivers. A woman who has made money one night is likely to attract attention the following day and likely to become the center of socialization that would take place around breakfast or lunch, or around the consumption of coffee, *chat* or drinks. A few days of observation were enough for me to see that a culture of sharing and of communalism is firmly established among the sex workers of Addis Ababa. It is also obvious that it is generated by the insecurities and uncertainties that surround the work that they do.

Although this culture of communalism is often not structured, there is almost always a structure that gives it the form of a transaction, by which I mean an exchange in which material transfers are made in anticipation of future reciprocation. Even if the resources flow in one direction and some friends appear to benefit at the expense of others, there is a deep-seated belief that a situation might be created tomorrow in which any one of them might have to draw upon her social capital. Sex work, as one of my informants (Tirusew) aptly put it, is a kind of work that has no other form of social security system; it is in her words, ታመው:የማይበላሽ (not life-sustaining [if one falls on bad times like] illness).

However, this culture of sharing and communalism is not equally established or uniformly practiced among the various categories of sex workers. There is a greater circulation of goods and cash among sex workers who work and live together than among those who work independently out of their homes. The asphalt women are therefore more communalistic than, say, the *bale-alga* or the *buna-bet* women.

The broadest social circle in the context of which sex workers of Addis Ababa come into contact with wider society is made of their neighbors. From interaction with neighbors, sex workers seek to establish channels through which they could have access to social or material resources that cannot be provided to them by individuals (be they family, kin, fellow sex workers or clients). The social resources that the women stand in need of might include protection against violence, support at times of illness or burial when death occurs. The material resources that they might obtain by drawing on their neighbors might include money and/or household goods of various kinds. Just as networking with different kinds of individuals is prompted by the desire to overcome the limitations imposed by the work itself and by poverty, networking with a community of neighbors is also prompted by the desire to ensure physical and social security.

Sex workers relate to their neighbors both formally and informally, that is, both individually in an *ad hoc* manner and institutionally through membership in social organizations. The informal *ad hoc* or individual interactions with neighbors take the form of social activities like visiting the sick, attending funerals or calling upon a bereaved neighbor, attending weddings or calling upon a neighbor who has announced some happy occasion. The formal interactions take the form of membership in community organizations like *idir* (a funerary association) and *iqub* (a sort of credit union). Both *idir* and *iqub* take various forms. *Idirs* range from the gender-specific dinner *idirs* that help assemble food items at the house of the bereaved member for several nights to neighborhood-wide associations (called *dinkwan idir*) that organize funerals and make financial contributions to the bereaved. Likewise, *iqub* types range from small pools in which a few friends contribute and collect money in turns to large pools in which the women join in with a variety of other people.

The statistics on the *idir* and *iqub* membership of sex workers in my sample indicate that though both institutions are made use of by the women, a much larger number of them prefer *iqubs* to the *idirs*. Out of my sample of 100 women, only 19 said that they are members of *idir*, whereas a significant 56% said that they are engaged in *iqub* with their neighbors on a regular basis. Interestingly, over 90% of the women who have *idir* said that they were admitted by their neighbors with full knowledge of their work in the sex business.

There is, however, a marked difference among the different categories of sex workers regarding membership in these neighborhood organizations. The sex workers who tend to join in *iqub* and *idir* are those who had a track record of long residence in the neighborhoods or those who head families. Thus, in my sample, the largest number of sex workers who said that they are members of *idir* came from the three categories that operate from the neighborhoods and which have relatively permanent venues of work: *bale-alga* (37%), the fixed-rate *akafay* (37%) and the *metet-bet* workers (21%). Only 5%of the women who work out of *buna-bet* said that they have *idir*.

Not surprisingly, none of my informants who work on the asphalt or out of the big hotels or nightclubs said that they have membership in neighborhood *idirs*. Equally not surprisingly, none of the women who work as equal-share *akafay* said that they have *idir*. These categories of sex workers, as I have pointed out above, tend to be mobile both in terms of venues of work and of residence. Even more interesting data comes when we look at the nature of the *idirs* in which the women are members. We see that only the *bale-alga*, the category of sex workers who are distinctive for their permanence in the neighborhoods, have joined in with non-sex workers in *idirs*. The *idirs* in which all the women who work as fixed-rate *akafay* are members are exclusively made up of the women themselves.

The figures on *iqub* showed a relatively similar pattern of correlation with the residence and types of work, although they are a little more inclusive of all types unlike *idir*. The largest percentage of women who regularly joined *iqubs* belong the two categories that are relatively settled, namely the *bale-alga* and the fixed-rate *akafay*. Together, the two categories constitute 58.4% of those who have *iqub*. The remainder was made up of asphalt workers (11%), hotels/nightclub workers (9.4%), equal-share *akafay* (5.6%) and *metet-bet* workers (1.8%). These distributions to some extent reflect the sub-cultures associated with each category of sex workers that I have mentioned earlier in this chapter and in the previous two chapters. The asphalt women in particular, but also the transient and mobile elements in the other categories, tend to spend money in their communalist living rather than save it. Interestingly, the predominant majority of *iqubs* in which sex workers are members were based on residence rather than gender, occupation or friendship. The distribution for my sample was 45% based on residence, 12% based on gender and 12 % based on friendship. None were based on occupation.

The differences between the figures for *idir* and *iqub* membership of sex workers prove two important points. The first is that, as long term community institutions, *idirs* require more permanent residence of the women than *iqubs*. Secondly, and equally importantly, *idir* membership is open by and large to women who are heads of households not just to any one known to be resident in the neighborhood. It is noteworthy, in this connection, that the fixed rate *akafay*, who are relatively permanent in terms of residence but who are not heads of the households in which they live and work, are organized in separate *idirs* of their own rather than with the community as a whole.

For the sex workers of Addis Ababa, interaction with neighbors (both formally and informally) could mean interacting with other sex workers or with non-sex-workers, or with both at the same time. This wide range of forms of interaction is made possible because sex work is not confined to specific localities in the city and is practiced in mixed settlements that combine residential homes with establishments related to sex work. Even in those localities that are known to house the largest number of sex workers, it is common to find residents who have nothing to do with sex work.

Yet, the form that the interaction between sex workers and their neighbors takes varies considerably depending on the proportion in which establishments related to sex-work are combined with residential homes. In those neighborhoods where sex work is widely practiced, the relationship between the sex worker and other people in the neighborhood tends to be smooth and integrative, while in those communities where sex

132

workers are few and far between the tendency is for them to be isolated or left out on a broad range of issues.

My informants who live in neighborhoods predominantly made up of sex workers were not only very happy about their relationship with their neighbors but are very categorical about the centrality of these relationships for their life. Almaz, who lives in the famous sex-worker neighborhood of *Katanga,* says the following:

> I have said to you that I don't have any relatives. All I have in this world is my daughter and my neighbors. To tell you the truth, my neighbors are everything for me. They are the only fall back that I have if something happens to me; they visit me when I fall ill; they lend me money if I am hard pressed for money; they come to my help if I am confronted by an intruder; and, I am sure, even though I do not have an *idir* because I can't afford to pay, they would give me a decent burial when I die.

In contrast to Almaz, Fantu G. lives in a house located in a compound that houses families that are not very happy about her work and is engaged in a continuous altercation with them about their security and well being. She laments her situation thus:

> Now, look at me here! I am in a difficult position due to the location of my house. I am neither a *bale-tidar* [a married woman] nor really a *shermuta* [sex worker]. While the latter is supposed to be what I do for a living, I am unable to make the most of it due to the way I live in this neighborhood. My neighbors would close the outside gate as early as 6 o'clock in the evening; they would not let me stand at the gate because, according to them, I will attract drunken people or other undesirable types to the compound. Honestly, I live here like a prisoner, hated by all my neighbors and hating everybody.

The form and content of social relationship between sex workers and their neighbors is also highly responsive to the type of sex work that is practiced by the women. Certain types of sex work appear to permit or encourage positive relationships with neighbors while other types discourage such relationship. Those types of sex work carried out from residences (like *be-alga*) are bound to take place in neighborhoods made predominantly of current or former sex workers. This results in a relatively easy integration of the women (like Almaz quoted above) into their immediate surroundings. On the other hand, types of sex work that are carried out from venues other than one's residence tend to limit or complicate the involvement of the sex workers with the community around their residence. This is the case, for instance, of women who are engaged in types of sex work like *asphalt*, *buna-bet*, nightclub, etc. Fantu H, who works on the streets, describes her relationship with neighbors as very difficult:

> We [she and her siblings] don't have a healthy relationship with our neighbors. I don't engage with them because I know that they talk behind my back about my working in this manner at this young age. I don't like their gossiping. I therefore discourage my sisters from interacting with them. Even if we are in dire economic need, we prefer to shut our doors and suffer alone.

A complicated situation arises in those anomalous cases where women who practice sex work at home (like Fantu G above) are surrounded by neighbors who have little to do with it or actually disapprove of it. This kind of situation makes for a very unstable and rancorous relationship between women and their neighbors.

I think it is fair to conclude from the foregoing that sex work in Addis Ababa sustains, and is in turn sustained by, a variety of social relationships that the women cultivate as part of their daily encounters with people they meet both at work and where they live. These social relationships are cultivated for two reasons: to make up for the social ties and interactions that had been disrupted because of engagement in sex work and to try and find an exit out of sex work. In other words, they are cultivated both to make life in commercial sex bearable and to find a way out of this life. Because women who have taken up commercial sex are, by definition, women who live in the most serious forms of economic adversity, it is a matter of daily struggle for them to determine just how much of their time, their energy or their money should be devoted to this kind of social existence and how much of it should go into sustaining them and their dependents materially.

Many women who spend money and time on building social networks do so because it is not possible to determine beforehand as to which kinds of social investment might provide an exit out of this line of work and which kinds would bring additional burdens on them. In fact, it is safe to assume that these networks have helped many women to get out of sex work eventually. Evidence from my interviews with currently practicing women confirms that they have enabled many women to exit sex work temporarily. 47% of the women in my sample say that they had quit sex work at one point and had returned to it later. For most of these women the exits were made possible through people with whom they came into contact while working as sex workers. Even if the exits do not come that frequently, however, there is no doubt that the network of friends, lovers and neighbors that the women build around them makes their life in sex work bearable.

4 Conclusion

In this chapter I have presented evidence to show that for the sex workers of Addis Ababa, engaging in commercial sex does not constitute withdrawal from society in any comprehensive sense. I have shown that, on the contrary, what it meant was that the women make a shift of focus and a conscious strategy to continue to live socially. I have argued that this shift of focus and strategy was necessary in part because sex work is never taken up at will or accepted as a permanent undertaking by the women who engage in it and in part because of the fact of poverty, which virtually all the women in commercial sex face. By presenting the words of the women themselves, I have shown that life as a sex worker in Addis Ababa is lived everyday by balancing one kind of morality (like the morality of materially helping family members and relatives under stress) against another kind of morality (sexual morality), and by balancing the reality of economic adversity with hope.

The struggle between morality and reality produces three distinct forms of relationship between the sex workers and people around them. In the first form, we see the women struggling to maintain their ties with family and kin. In the second, we see them trying to protect existing ties from disintegrating by avoiding contact with family and kin who are believed to have reasons of their own not to accept the women's involvement in commercial sex. In the third form we see the women

135

building a network of new relationships both to reduce the pain and agony of life as sex workers and to find ways of getting out of it.

These are not mutually exclusive options, necessarily. All women who make a living through commercial sex try to combine them as much as possible. Some combine the options successfully while others are compelled by circumstances to focus on one or another. The variables that determine these degrees of success are the variables that I have used for the classification of the women, namely: socioeconomic background, manners of entry into sex work, place and conditions of work, place and conditions of residence and the relationship of dependence that the women had gotten into both before and after becoming sex workers.

Chapter Six

Conclusions and Policy Considerations

The existing literature on sex work in Ethiopia shares a number of characteristics with the literature on the same topic elsewhere in Africa as well as outside of the continent. Among these widely shared characteristics is the portrayal of sex workers either as social misfits who pollute society or as victims who are abused by patriarchy. The literature falls into two broad categories on the basis of which of these two portrayals of women the writers have chosen. One of them, to which I refer as male-centered, portrays sex workers as socially deprived people who represent a moral affront to society. The other, to which I refer as female-centered, portrays them as women who are paying for the crimes of a male-biased social order by taking their bodies to the market. In this study I have called attention to the fact that both of these portrayals were developed in the context of Western European experiences and that they reflected ethnographic bias and ideological polarity among European scholars, social activists and public decision-makers. Some of the major shortcomings of the African (and also Ethiopian) literature were consequences of taking over the paradigms developed for Western European societies without making allowances for the very significant differences between the two types of societies in social structure as well as culture.

The Africanist (and Ethiopianist) literature has borrowed a number of other things from this Euro-centric literature. One of these is the tendency to portray the women collectively and categorically. For those who take the male-centered perspectives, the women are, *one and all,* a social liability, with no internal differentiation. Likewise, for those who take the female-centered perspectives, the women are, *one and all,* victims of gender discrimination by society. I have argued that neither of these categorical approaches is correct because they tend to impose identities of one kind or another on the women, identities that are too sweeping and too simplistic.

The other characteristic that the African (and the Ethiopian) literature on sex work has borrowed from the Western literature has to do with methodology. Prior to the development of the Women's Movement, the

137

literature on sex work in Europe had employed methodologies that took female sex workers as objects rather than subjects of social research. Views about the women held by thinkers and scholars were believed to be more important than views held by the women about themselves and the world around them.

In this work, I have attempted to overcome the limitations that I have pointed out above. I have thus sought, first, to identify the criteria with which we can arrive at a meaningful breakdown of the sex worker population as part of an attempt to understand the experiences of the women as differentiated experiences. The identification of these criteria benefited from previous works on the institution of commercial sex in Ethiopia (notably those of Laketch Dirasse and Andargachew Tesfaye) but also involved seeking additional variables that I thought would add new perspectives and insights. I have also sought to adopt a research methodology that brings to the center stage the perspectives of sex workers themselves.

My conscious effort to look at sex work as a differentiated phenomenon and to base my insights on the perspectives of the women themselves has produced some points which I believe are important to formulate a wise and practical approach to the phenomenon of commercial sex in Addis Ababa. The first point is that, unlike the situation a few decades ago, the sex trade in Addis Ababa has increasingly become an occupation of women who are born and brought up in the city. What this means is that the causative factors behind the expansion of commercial sex recently have to be sought from within the city rather than from outside of it. The growing predominance of intra-city sex work shows itself, among other things, in the organization of sex-related work in all the different venues. In most of the venues, sex workers who constitute the resident, permanent, or relatively immobile elements tend to have been immigrants to the city whereas those who constitute the non-resident, transient and mobile elements tend to have been non-immigrants.

The second point that has emerged from my attempt to combine differentiation with insider perspectives is that the sociology of sex work is directly and indirectly related to control over space, both in-door space and out-door space. Control over housing is the primary element in determining who works for whom and who benefits from the labor of the women. Those who hold titles to houses or buildings suited for commercial sex, be it in the slums and back alleys of the city or along its major streets, determine the conditions of work indoors; likewise, the strong men of the streets, who can manipulate or control the dangerous underworld, determine the conditions of work outdoors. What we have, as a result, is a class of entrepreneurs that are tied to sex work, not just indirectly through its association with liquor trade, etc., but also directly through control over sexual services. The other context, again related to housing, in which non-sex workers control income from commercial sex is the context of residence. Commercial sex workers make arrangements of residence that are distinctively suited to the types of work they do. In most of them, they have to submit to arrangements that allocate considerable material benefits to those who hold titles to the houses while denying the women the minimal conditions for privacy and decent living.

The third point is that, women who practice commercial sex are highly differentiated not only in terms of their social background, age, education, etc but also in terms of the type of commercial sex work in which they engage; that they include among them women who perform tasks of social reproduction as heads of families or as breadwinners; that almost all of them maintain social ties and carry social obligations of the kind that society appreciates and values very highly. In other words, the women who engage in commercial sex and those that do not engage in it are united not just in the fact of being women but also (and significantly so) in their diversity. I am convinced that this view is more useful than many currently popular views for strategies that society might want to devise in order to reduce or limit commercial sex and deal with the many problems associated with it.

For instance, it is difficult and in fact incorrect to talk about commercial sex workers collectively with regard to HIV/AIDS. The degree as well as forms of vulnerability of commercial sex workers to HIV depends, among other things, on the type of sex work that the women do. My study revealed that there were types of sex work that make the women particularly vulnerable to HIV infections and other types that permit them to be relatively less vulnerable.

In connection with HIV/AIDS, the other finding of the research is that commercial sex workers become more vulnerable to HIV in their non paying relation with men than their paying/commercial relation with men. It is usually assumed that commercial sex workers become vulnerable to HIV in their paying/commercial sexual relation with men (i.e. in their sexual relation with men who come to buy sexual service). But the research suggests that this is only half the story. There are intimate people whom the women call lovers, friends and husbands. These people have unrestricted and almost always unprotected sexual access to the women. These kinds of arrangements are common among the asphalt sex workers who usually have pimps. In return for their protection, these men get from the women among other things free and unprotected sexual service.

The fourth point that comes out of my study is what I have called the humane approach towards commercial sex workers. Commercial sex is an occupation in which women find themselves unwillingly. What this means is that public or official perceptions that this is what the women choose to do are misplaced. A clear distinction should be made between commercial sex as an occupation and the women who are engaged in it. It is important to factor this element in all kinds of initiatives at all levels of municipal government. It is also significant to work towards increasing public awareness about it.

The fifth point is that mistreatment in the hands of domestic employers has been one of the most frequently reported reasons for eventually turning into commercial sex. So it is important to explore the ways in which domestic labor can be regulated in the urban context. It is also important to monitor the activities of the brokers who encourage women to take up sex work.

Lastly, it is important to consider intra-gender affirmative action initiatives. Affirmative action has often been understood in the generic sense, in the sense of expanding opportunities for women in general. This perception often ignores that there are poor women who suffer from particularly severe forms of economic and social marginalization. Enabling women in general should be pursued through enabling particularly disadvantaged women. Initiatives in this area might include programs to create gainful employment opportunities for former sex workers. It might also include reserving certain areas of employment in publicly funded projects for women who come from this category.

Aklilu, M.1998. "Factors associated with HIV Infection Among Sex Workers of Addis Ababa, Ethiopia". M.Ph. Thesis: Department of Community Health, Addis Ababa University.

Alemayehu Bisrat. 1996. "Is Prostitution the Last Resort? Case Study of Prostitutes in Two *Kebeles* of Addis Ababa". BA Thesis, Sociology, Addis Ababa University.

Alemayehu Mekuria. 1973. "Urbanization as a Major Factor that Contributes to the Spread of Prostitution in Addis Ababa". BA Thesis, Haile Selassie I University, School of Social Work.

Andargatchew Tesfaye. 1967. The Problem of Prostitution in Ethiopia, in *Alumni Association Bulletin,* Addis Ababa.

----------------------------1988. "The Crime Problem and its Correction" (Unpublished), Department of Sociology and Social Administration, Addis Ababa University.

Assefa Damte. 1993. "Urbanization in Ethiopia: Pre and Post Revolution Experiences". Ph.D. Dissertation, Urban Studies, the University of Wisconsin-Milwaukee.

Atakilt G.Yohannes.1994. "The Attitude of Bar Maids Towards AIDS/HIV Prevention: A Case Study of 30 Bar Maids in A Few Selected Bars around Piazza". Senior Essay in Sociology, Addis Ababa University.

Ayehunie S.1987. "Prevalence of anti-HIV Antibodies in Prostitutes and their Clients in Addis Ababa". M.Sc. Thesis, Department of Biology, Addis Ababa University.

Baardson, P. 1993. "Child Prostitution in Addis Ababa: Survey and Background" Report Prepared for Radda Barnen.

Bakwesegha, C.J. 1982. *Profiles of Urban Prostitution: A Case Study From Uganda.* Nairobi, Kenya Literature Bureau.

Banchiyeleku Gebreyes. 1984. "A Survey on Causes of Prostitution in Higher 1 Kebele 07 (Addis Ababa). BA Thesis, Applied Sociology, Addis Ababa University.

Barry, K. 1981a. "The Underground Economic System of Pimping", Journal of International Affairs, Vol. 35, (1): 10-17.

1981b. Female *Sexual Slavery.* New York, New York University Press.

---

[2] Ethiopian names have been entered generally by first name rather than by father's name.

1984. *International Feminism: Networking Against Female Sexual Slavery*. New York. International Women's Tribune Center.

Bethlehem Tekola. 2002. *Narratives of Three Prostitutes in Addis Ababa.* CERTWID: Addis Ababa University.

------------------------2003. *"How Should Prostitution be Dealt With? CERTWID Informs*, Vol.7, no.3 (November, 2003).

------------------------2004. "Sex Workers in Day Light: the Social Context of Sex Work in Addis Ababa". MA Thesis: Department of Sociology and Social Anthropology, Addis Ababa University.

------------------------2004. "Youth and HIV/AIDS in Addis Ababa: Perspectives on the Interface between Commercial Sex and HIV/AIDS", *CERTWID Informs*, Vol. 9, no.2 (August, 2004).

Bujra, J. 1975. "Women 'Entrepreneurs' of Early Nairobi", *Canadian Journal of African Studies*, vol.9, no. 2: 213-34.

Chodorow, N. 1978. The Reproduction of Mothering, Psychoanalysis and the Sociology of Gender. Berkeley, University of California Press.

Cohen, A. 1969. *Custom and Politics: A Study of Hausa Migrants in Yoruba Towns*, Berkeley and Los Angeles: University of California Press.

De Beauvoir, S. 1974. *The Second Sex*, Harmondsworth, Penguin Books.

Emecheta, B. 1979. The Joys of Motherhood. New York, George Braziller.

Gedu Anbesse. 1995. "A Case Study of Five Bar Maids on their Situation and Attitude Toward
  Rehabilitation". BA Thesis, Addis Ababa University.

Girma Seifu Maru. 1997. "Poverty in Addis Ababa: A Comparison of Female and Male headed
      Households". MA Thesis, Addis Ababa University.

Habtamu Workie. 1991. "An Assessment of Prostitutes of Akakie Awraja Industrial Zone". BA Thesis in Sociology and Social Administration, Addis Ababa University.

Heyl, B.S. 1979. *The Madame as Entrepreneur: Career management in House Prostitution*. New Brunswick, New Jersey, Transaction Books.

Huppert, G. 1986. *After the Black Death: A Social History of Early Modern Europe.*Bloomington and Indianapolis, Indiana University Press.

142

Hussein M.1998. "HIV-1 Subtype C in Commercial Sex Workers in Addis Ababa, Ethiopia". M.Sc. Thesis, Department of Community Health, Addis Ababa University.

Jaget, C. 1980. Prostitutes – *Our Life*. Bristol, Falling Wall Press.

Jaggar, A.1983. *Feminist Politics and Human Nature*. Sussex, Harvester Press.

Kebede Mirra. 1993. "The Prevalence of HIV Infection and Its Impact on Prostitutes". Senior Essay in Sociology, Addis Ababa University.

Kebede Yeshitla. 1980. "A Study of Some Aspects of Prostitution in Keftegna Two". Senior Essay in Sociology, Addis Ababa University.

Laketch Dirasse. 1978. "The Socioeconomic Position of Women in Addis Ababa: the Case of Prostitution". PhD Dissertation, Boston University.

--------------------1991. *The Commoditization of Female Sexuality: Prostitution and Socio-Economic Relations in Addis Ababa, Ethiopia*. New York: AMS Press.

LaPin, D. 1984. "Women in African Literature" in Hay, M.J and Stichter, S, eds. *African Women South of the Sahara*. London and New York: Longman.

Laslett, P. 1965. *The World We Have Lost: England Before the Industrial Age*. New York.

Lema Gutema.1968. "The Problem of Prostitution in the Urban Areas of Ethiopia" (Unpublished) Addis Ababa University.

Lishan Tenagashaw. 1985. "An Assessment of the Psycho-Social and Vocational Training of the Prostitutes of the Gullele Rehabilitation Center". Senior Essay, Department of Sociology and Social Administration, Addis Ababa University.

Malos, E. (ed.).1980. *The Politics of Housework*. London, Allison and Busby.

Mayor, H.1962. "Prostitution and Venereal Diseases in Addis Ababa" (unpublished) Addis Ababa University.

-------------1963. "The problem of Venereal Diseases in Ethiopia" (unpublished) Addis Ababa University.

McLeod, E. 1982. *Women Working: Prostitution Now*. London, Croom Helm.

Mehret Mengestu, et.al. 1990. Sexual Behavior and Some Social Features Workers in the City of Addis Ababa. *The Ethiopian Journal of Health Development,* 4 (2).

Mihiretu Belay. 1984. "The Causes and Impact of Divorce on Urban Life in Ethiopia". Senior Essay in Sociology and Social Administration, Addis Ababa University.

Mullings, L. 1976. "Women and Economic Change in Africa", in Hafkin and Bay, eds. *Women in Africa: Studies in Social and Economic Change*. Stanford: Stanford University Press.

Mulumebet Zenebe. 2000. "Female Prostitution in Addis Ababa: Problems and Future Directions". A Summary Report Prepared foe A Research Outcome Dissemination Workshop, Addis Ababa University.

O' Neill, M. 1996. "Prostitution, Feminism and Critical Praxis: Profession Prostitute?" In *The Austrian Journal of Sociology*, Special edition on Work and Society.

Parrinder, G. 1980. *Sex in the World's Religions*. London, Sheldon Press.

Patterson, Orlando. 1982. *Slavery and Social Death*. Cambridge: Harvard University Press.

Phoenix, J. 1999. *Making Sense of Prostitution*. New York, Palgrave.

Rosenblum, K. E. 1975. "Female Deviance and the Female Sex Role: A Preliminary Investigation", *British Journal of Sociology*. Vol.26, (2): 169-85.

Seble Negussie. 1998. "Child Prostitution: The Study of 15 Child Prostitutes in Merkato" [Addis Ababa] BA Thesis, Sociology and Social Administration, Addis Ababa University.

Stearns, P. N. 1977. *The Face of Europe*. St. Louis, Forum Press.

Tamene Geremew. 1993. "A Case Study of 20 Prostitutes in Keftegna 5, Kebeles 06 and 12 in Addis Ababa". BA Thesis in Sociology, Addis Ababa University.

Tesfahunegn Wolde. 1990. "The Impact of AIDS on the Income of Prostitutes in Addis Ababa". Senior Essay in Sociology, Addis Ababa University.

Tobias, J.J. 1972. *Crime and Industrial Society in the Nineteenth Century*, London.

Truong, T. 1990. *Sex, Money and Morality: Prostitution and Tourism in Southeast Asia*. London and New Jersey, Zed Books Ltd.

Van Onselen. 1982. *Studies in the Social and Economic History of the Witwatersrand 1886-1914, 1: New Babylon*, London: Longman.

White, L. (1990). *The Comforts of Home: Prostitution in Colonial Nairobi*. Chicago, University of Chicago Press.

Yassin Worku. 1997. "Poverty in Addis Ababa: A Case Study of Selected Kebeles in Eastern Addis Ababa. MA Thesis in Geography, Addis Ababa University.

FSS Publications List

FSS Periodical

- *Medrek, now renamed FSS BULLETIN* (Quarterly since 1998. English and Amharic)

- *Africa Review of Books* (Managed by FSS for CODESRIA)
    - Vol. 1, No. 1 (October 2004)
    - Vol. 2, No. 2 (September 2005)

FSS Discussion Papers

No. 1 *Water Resource Development in Ethiopia: Issues of Sustainability and Participation.* Dessalegn Rahmato. 1999

No. 2 *The City of Addis Ababa: Policy Options for the Governance and Management of a City with Multiple Identity.* Meheret Ayenew. 1999

No. 3 *Listening to the Poor: A Study Based on Selected Rural and Urban Sites in Ethiopia.* Aklilu Kidanu and Dessalegn Rahmato. 2000

No. 4 *Small-Scale Irrigation and Household Food Security. A Case Study from Central Ethiopia.* Fuad Adem. 2001

No. 5 *Land Redistribution and Female-Headed Households.* Yigremew Adal. 2001

No. 6 *Environmental Impact of Development Policies in Peripheral Areas: The Case of Metekel, Northwest Ethiopia.* Wolde-Selassie Abbute. Forthcoming, 2001

No. 7 *The Environmental Impact of Small-scale Irrigation: A Case Study.* Fuad Adem. Forthcoming, 2001

No. 8 *Livelihood Insecurity Among Urban Households in Ethiopia.* Dessalegn Rahmato and Aklilu Kidanu. 2002

No. 9 *Rural Poverty in Ethiopia: Household Case Studies from North Shewa.* Yared Amare. 2002

No.10 *Rural Lands in Ethiopia: Issues, Evidences and Policy Response.* Tesfaye Teklu. 2003

No.11 *Resettlement in Ethiopia: The Tragedy of Population Relocation in the 1980s.* Dessalegn Rahmato. 2003

No.12 *Searching for Tenure Security? The Land System and New Policy Initiatives in Ethiopia.* Dessalegn Rahmato. 2004.

FSS Monograph Series

No. 1 *Survey of the Private Press in Ethiopia: 1991-1999.* Shimelis Bonsa. 2000

No. 2 *Environmental Change and State Policy in Ethiopia: Lessons from Past Experience.* Dessalegn Rahmato. 2001

No. 3 *Democratic Assistance to Post-Conflict Ethiopia: Impact and Limitations.* Dessalegn Rahmato and Meheret Ayenew. 2004

No. 4 *Lord, Zega and Peasant: A Study of Property and Agrarian Relations in Rural Eastern Gojjam.* Habtamu Mengistie. *2004.*

FSS Conference Proceedings

1. *Issues in Rural Development. Proceedings of the Inaugural Workshop of the Forum for Social Studies, 18 September 1998.* Edited by Zenebework Taddesse. 2000

2. *Development and Public Access to Information in Ethiopia.* Edited by Zenebework Tadesse. 2000

3. *Environment and Development in Ethiopia.* Edited by Zenebework Tadesse. 2001

4. *Food Security and Sustainable Livelihoods in Ethiopia.* Edited by Yared Amare. 2001

5. *Natural Resource Management in Ethiopia.* Edited by Alula Pankhurst. 2001

6. *Poverty and Poverty Policy in Ethiopia.* Special Issue. Papers presented at FSS conference on poverty, 8 March 2002, Addis Ababa

Consultation Papers on Poverty

No. 1 *The Social Dimensions of Poverty.* Minas Hiruy, Abebe Kebede, and Zenebework Tadesse. Edited by Meheret Ayenew. 2001

No. 2 *NGOs and Poverty Reduction.* Fassil W. Mariam, Abowork Haile, Berhanu Geleto, and Jemal Ahmed. Edited by Meheret Ayenew. 2001

No. 3 *Civil Society Groups and Poverty Reduction.* Abonesh H. Mariam, Zena Berhanu, and Zewdie Shitie. Edited by Meheret Ayenew. 2001

No. 4 *Listening to the Poor.* Oral Presentation by Gizachew Haile, Senait Zenawi, Sisay Gessesse and Martha Tadesse. In Amharic. Edited by Meheret Ayenew. 2001

No. 5 *The Private Sector and Poverty Reduction [Amharic].* Teshome Kebede, Mullu Solomon and Hailemeskel Abebe. Edited by Meheret Ayenew, 2001

No. 6 *Government, Donors and Poverty Reduction.* Mekonnen Manyazewal, William James Smith and Jeroen Verheul. Edited by Meheret Ayenew. 2002.

No. 7 *Poverty and Poverty Policy in Ethiopia.* Edited by Meheret Ayenew, 2002

Books

1. *Ethiopia: The Challenge of Democracy from Below*. Edited by Bahru Zewde and Siegfried Pausewang. Nordic African Institute, Uppsala and the Forum for Social Studies, Addis Ababa. 2002

Thematic Briefing

- *Thematic Briefings on Natural Resource Management*. Enlarged Edition. Edited by Alula Pankhurst. Produced jointly by the Forum for Social Studies and the University of Sussex. January 2001

Gender Policy Dialogue Series

No. 1 *Gender and Economic Policy*. Edited by Zenebework Tadesse. 2003
No. 2 *Gender and Poverty* (Amharic). Edited by Zenebework Tadesse. 2003
No. 3 *Gender and Social Development in Ethiopia*. (Forthcoming).
No. 4 *Gender Policy Dialogue in Oromiya Region*. Edited by Eshetu Bekele. 2003
No. 6 *Gender Policy Dialogue in Southern Region*. Edited by Eshetu Bekele. 2004.

Consultation Papers on Environment

No. 1 *Environment and Environmental Change in Ethiopia*. Edited by Gedion Asfaw. Consultation Papers on Environment. 2003
No. 2 *Environment, Poverty and Gender*. Edited by Gedion Asfaw. Consultation Papers on Environment. 2003
No. 3 *Environmental Conflict*. Edited by Gedion Asfaw. Consultation Papers on Environment. July 2003
No. 4 *Economic Development and its Environmental Impact*. Edited by Gedion Asfaw. Consultation Papers on Environment. 2003
No. 5 *Government and Environmental Policy*. Consultation Papers on Environment. 2004
No. 6 * የግልና የጋራ ጥረት ለአካባቢ ሕይወት መሻሻል (የስሜን ሸዋ ገበሬዎች ተሞክሮ)* Consultation Papers on Environment. May 2004
No. 7 *Promotion of Indigenous Trees and Biodiversity Conservation*. Consultation Papers on Environment. 2004

FSS Studies on Poverty

No. 1 *Some Aspects of Poverty in Ethiopia: Three Selected Papers.* Dessalegn Rahmato, Meheret Ayenew and Aklilu Kidanu. Edited by Dessalegn Rahmato. 2003.

No. 2 *Faces of Poverty: Life in Gäta, Wälo.* Harald Aspen. 2003.

No. 3 *Destitution in Rural Ethiopia.* Yared Amare. 2003

No. 4 *Environment, Poverty and Conflict.* Tesfaye Teklu and Tesfaye Tafesse. 2004

No. 5 *Issues in Urban Poverty: Two Selected Papers.* Daniel Kassahun and Meron Assefa. July 2005

ከድህነት ወደ ልማት፡- ዕውቀትን ለተውልድ ማስተላለፍ

ቁጥር 1: *ድርቅንና ረሀብን ለመቋቋም የተደረጉ እንቅስቃሴዎች (1966-1983)፡፡* ሺመልስ አዱኛ፣ 1997 ዓ.ም.

ቁጥር 2: *የአባይና የተፋሰሶቹ ዓለም ዓቀፋዊ ችግር፡፡* ዘውዴ ገ/ሥላሴ፣ 1997 ዓ.ም.

Environmental Documentaries on CD and Video

o የከተማችን አካባቢ ከተት ወደየት? (Amharic Video Film)

o ውጥንቅጥ፣ ድህነትና የአካባቢያችን መጎሳቆል (Amharic Video Film)

o "Witinkit": Poverty and Environmental Degradation (CD in Amharic with English Subtitles)

www.ingramcontent.com/pod-product-compliance
Lightning Source LLC
Chambersburg PA
CBHW020003290326
41935CB00007B/288